Shetland Pony Coloring Book for Adults

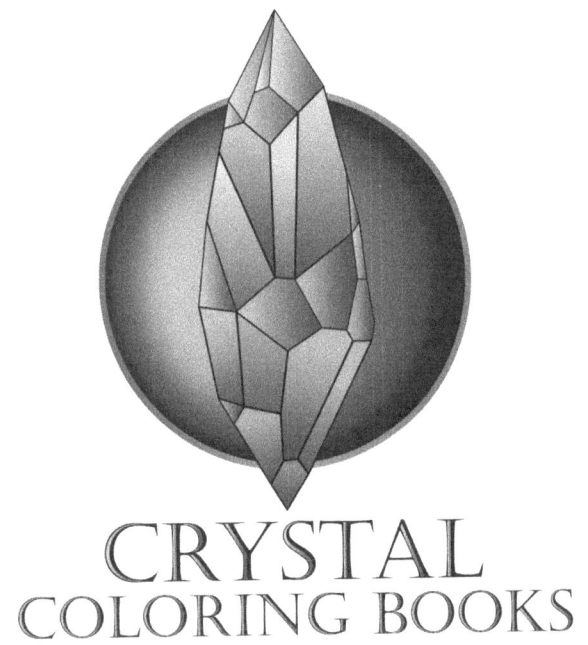

Crystal Coloring Books

Copyright © 2018 Crystal Coloring Books
All rights reserved.

ISBN: 9781729372692

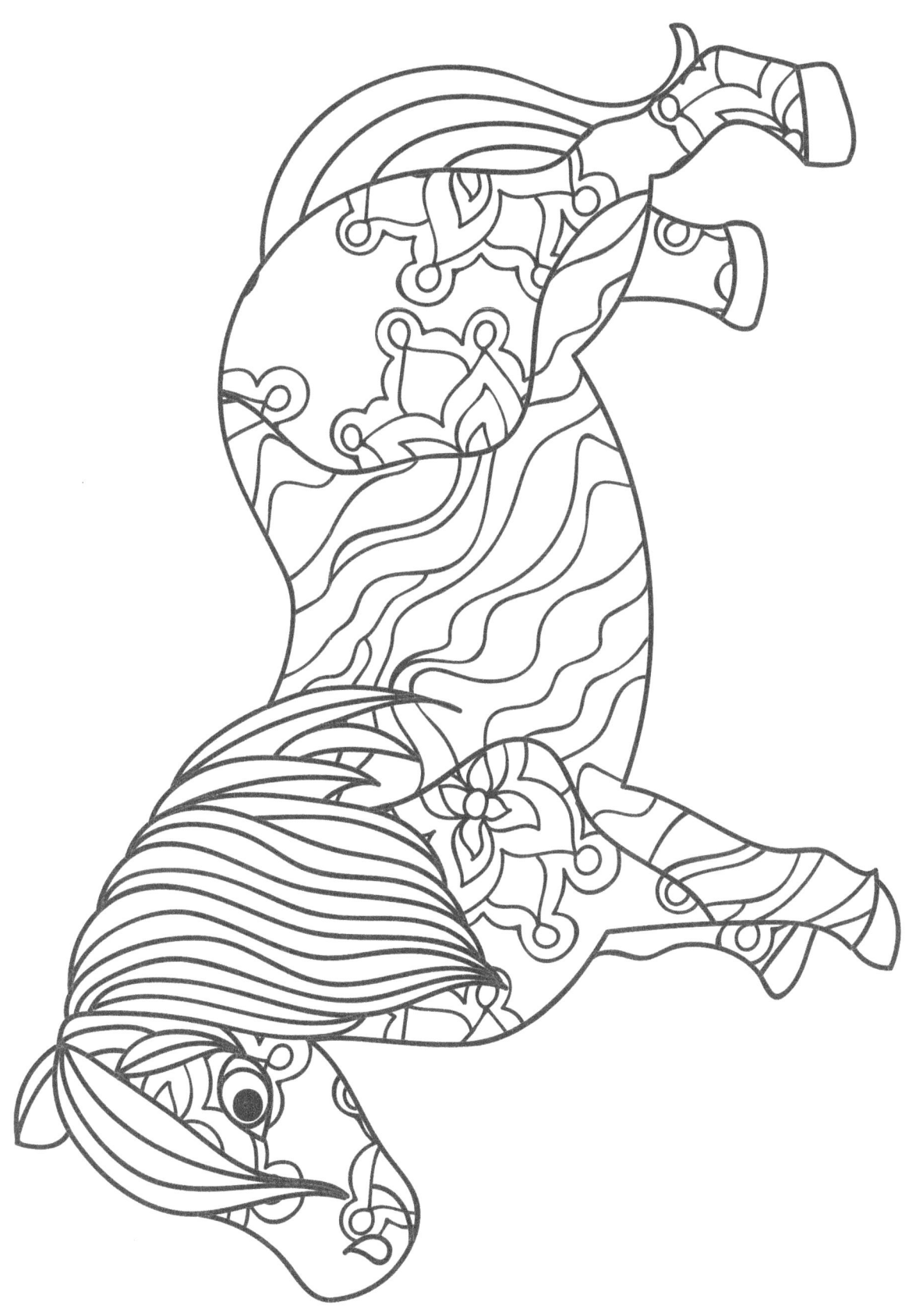

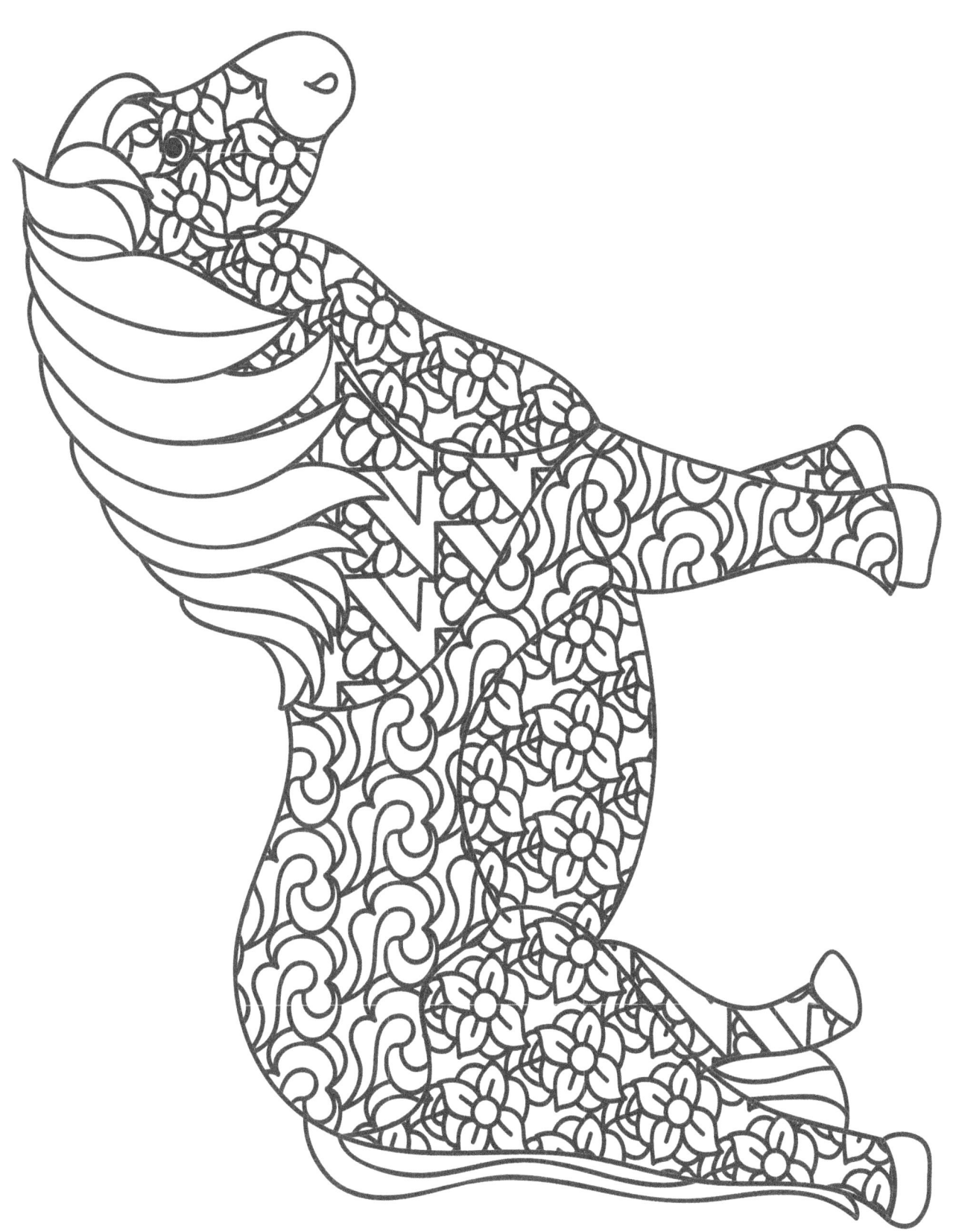

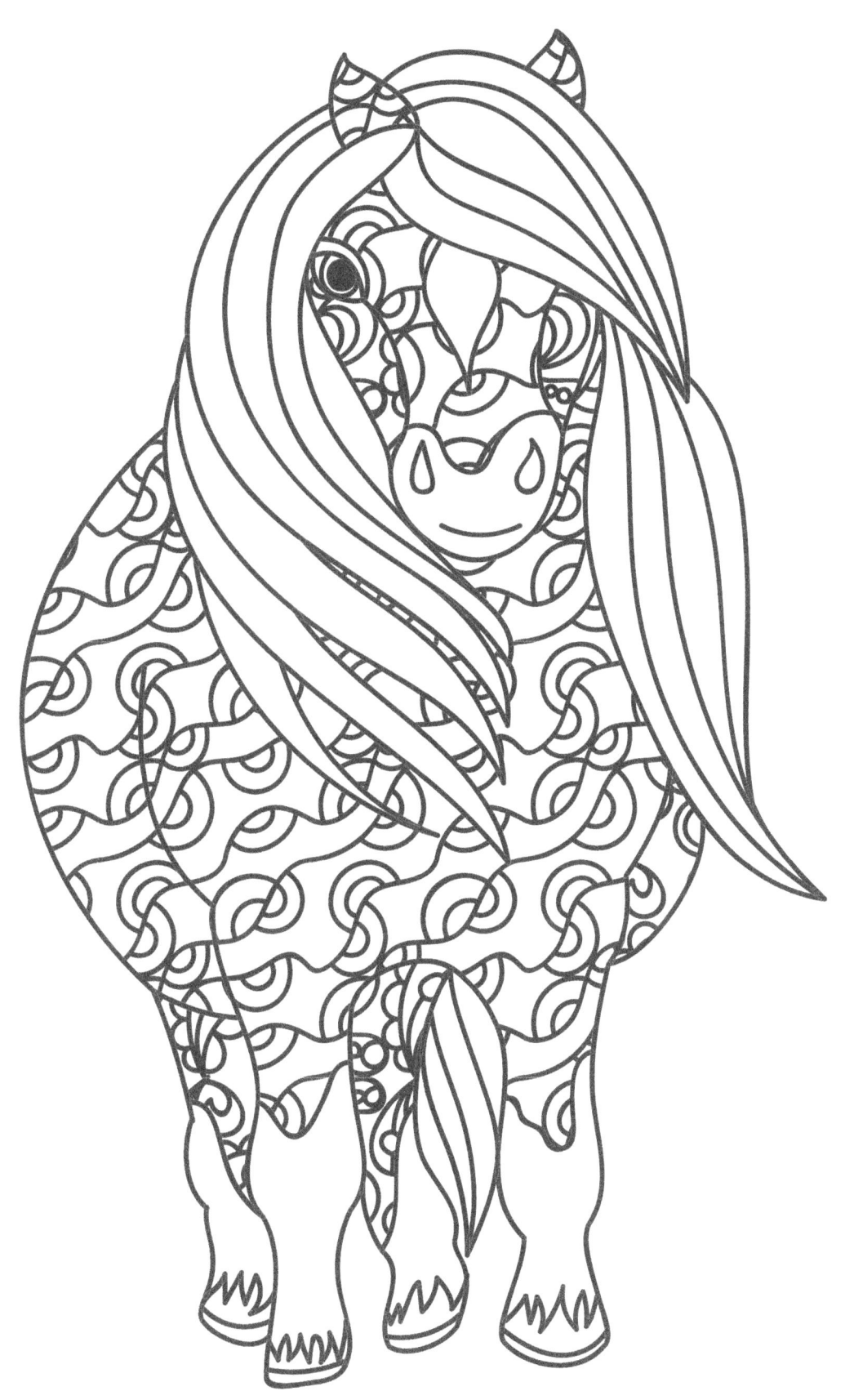

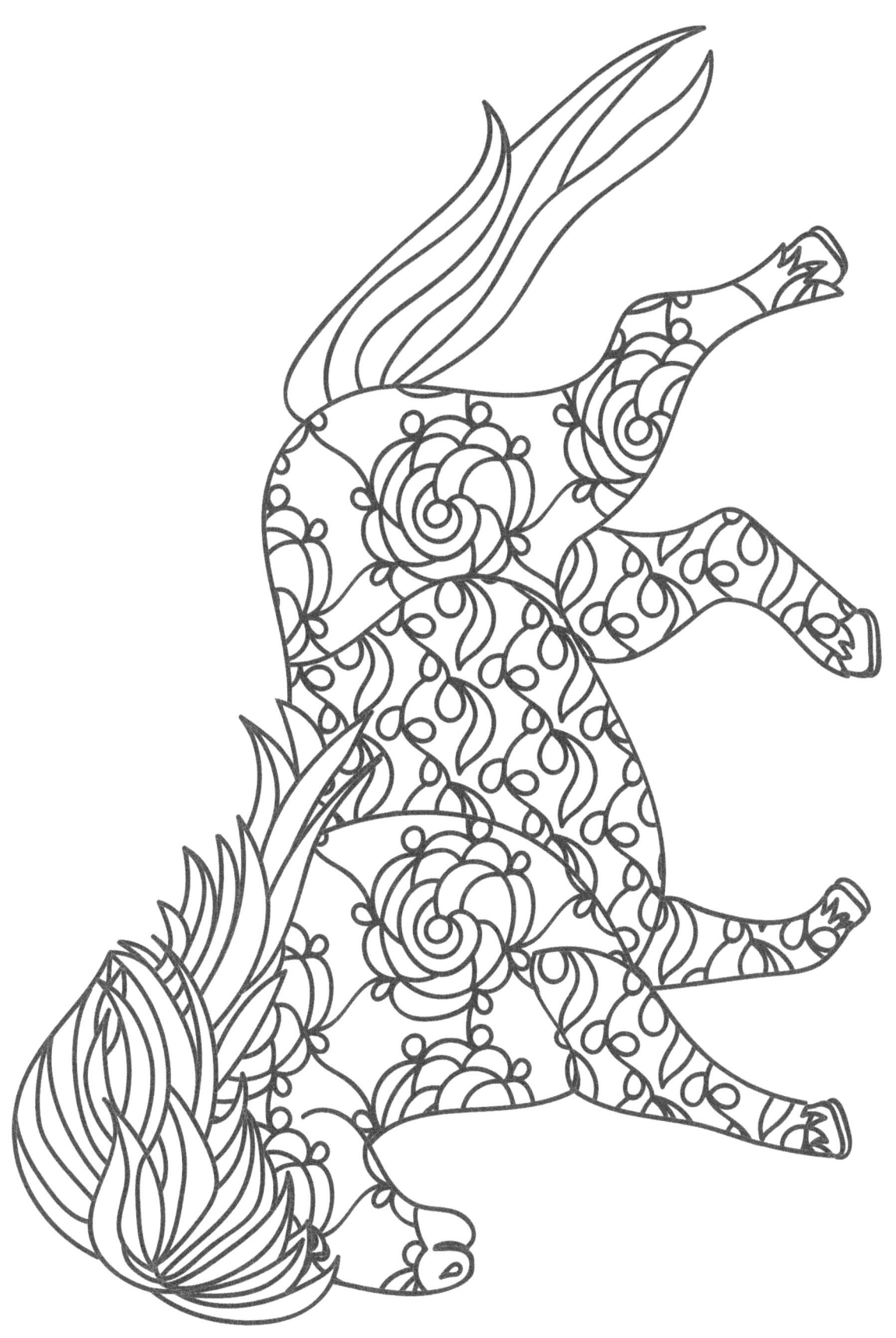

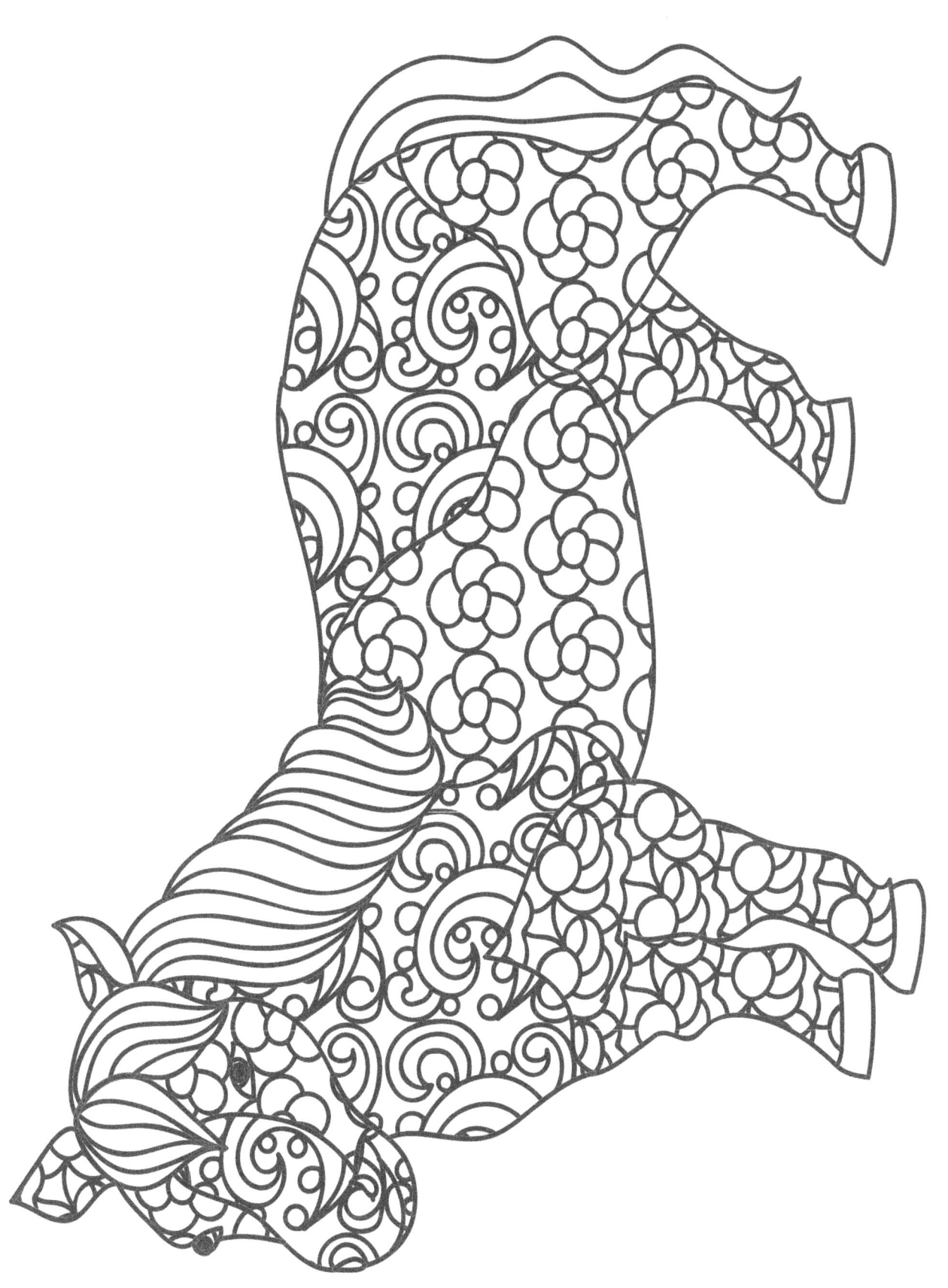

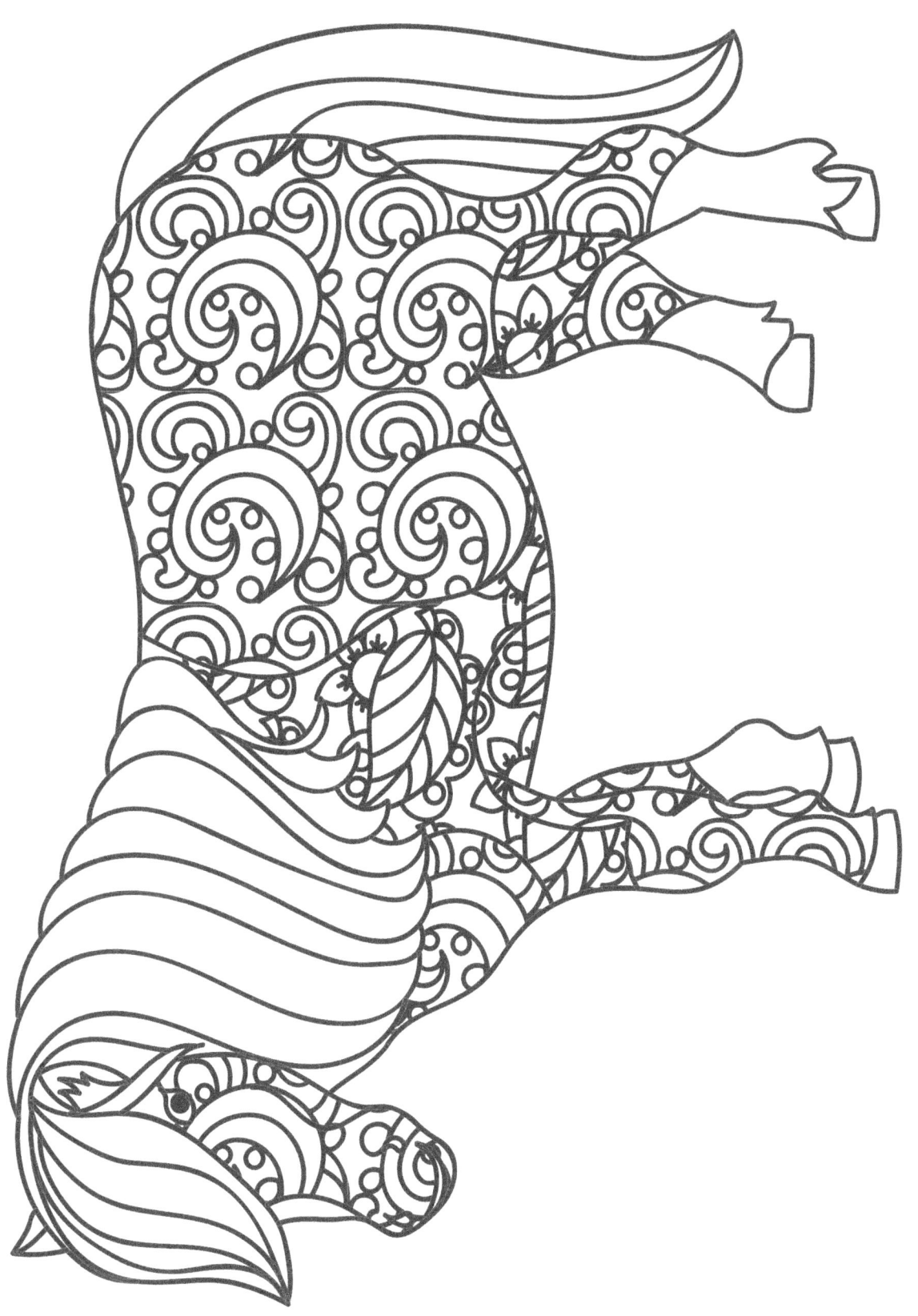

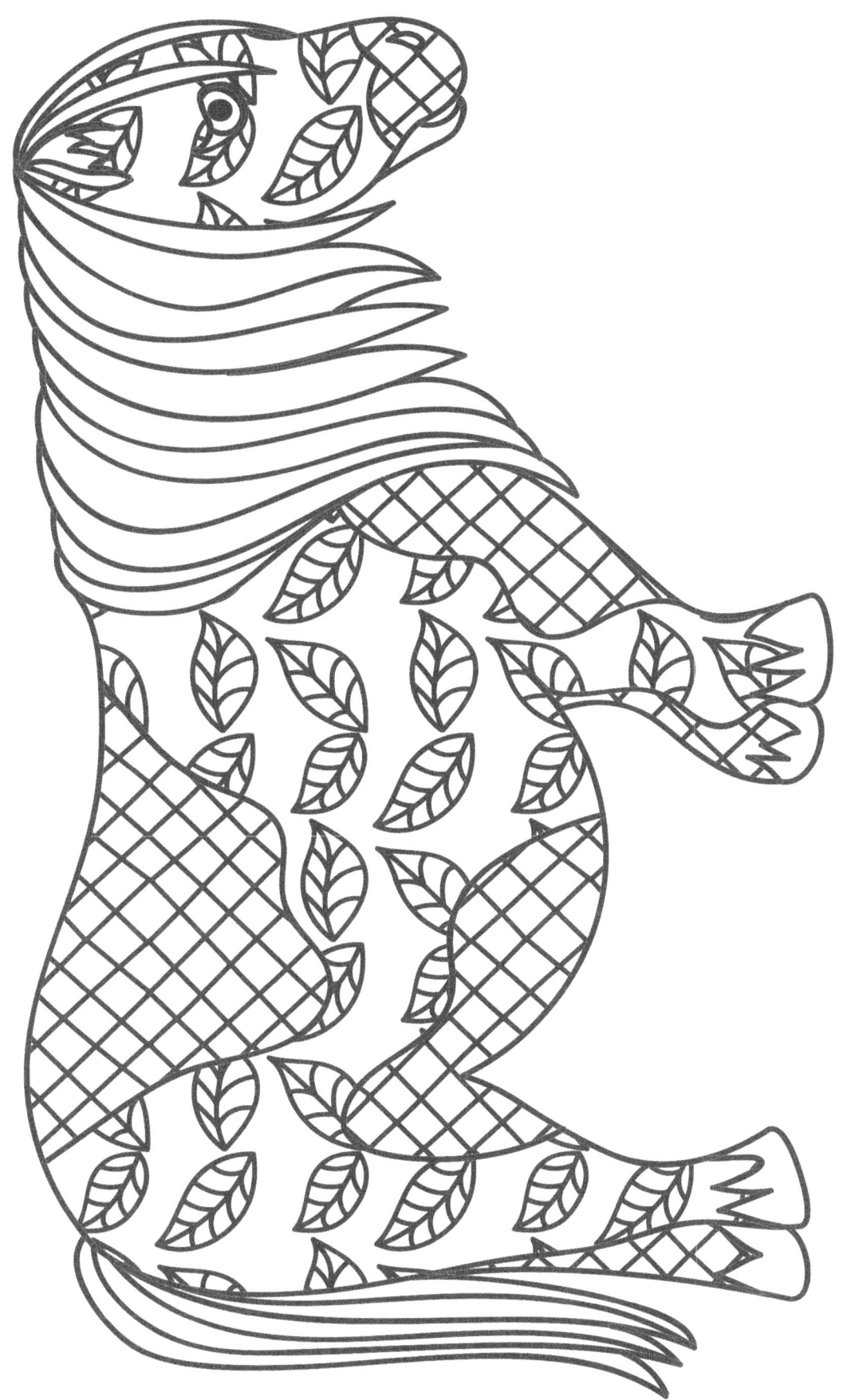

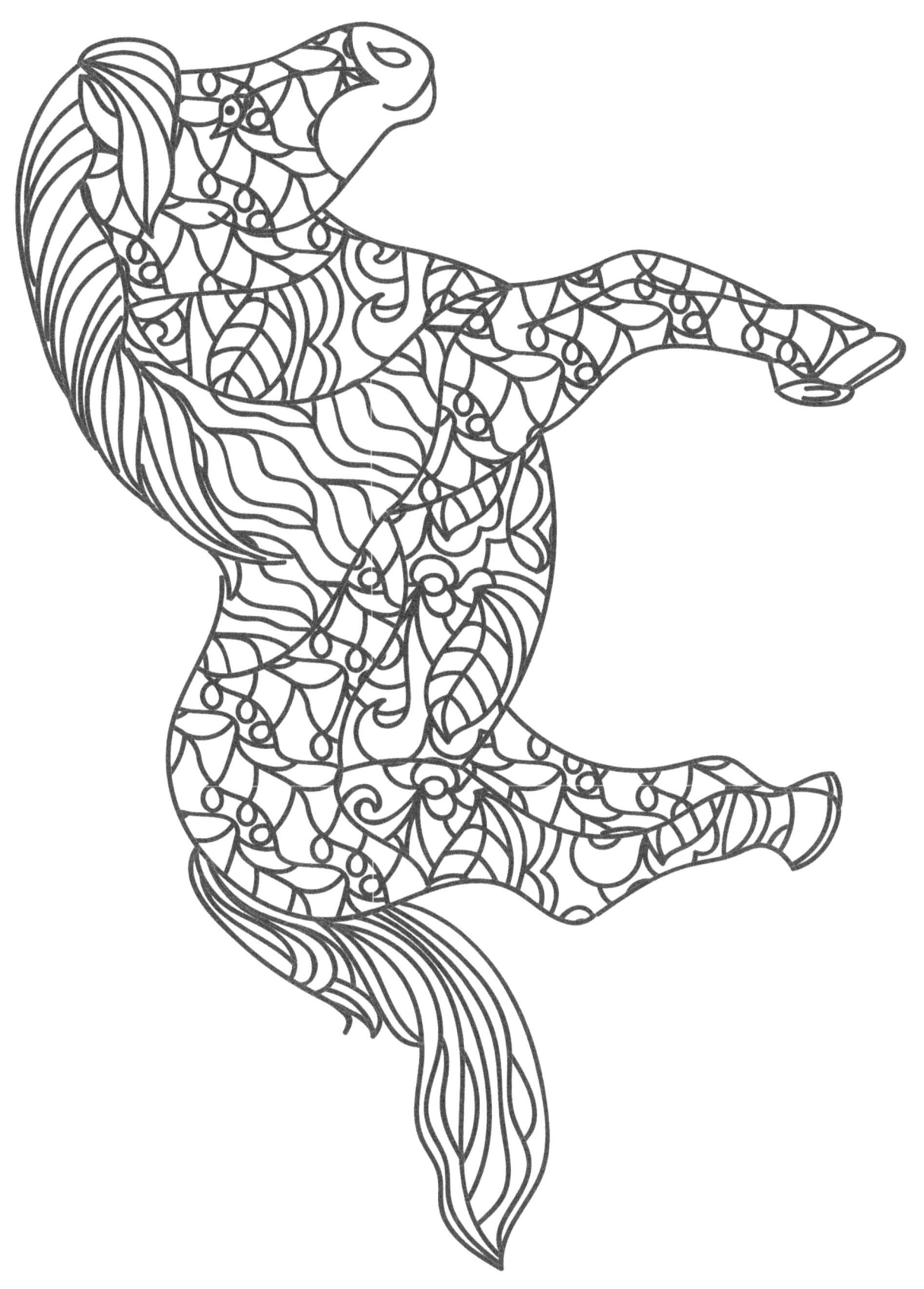

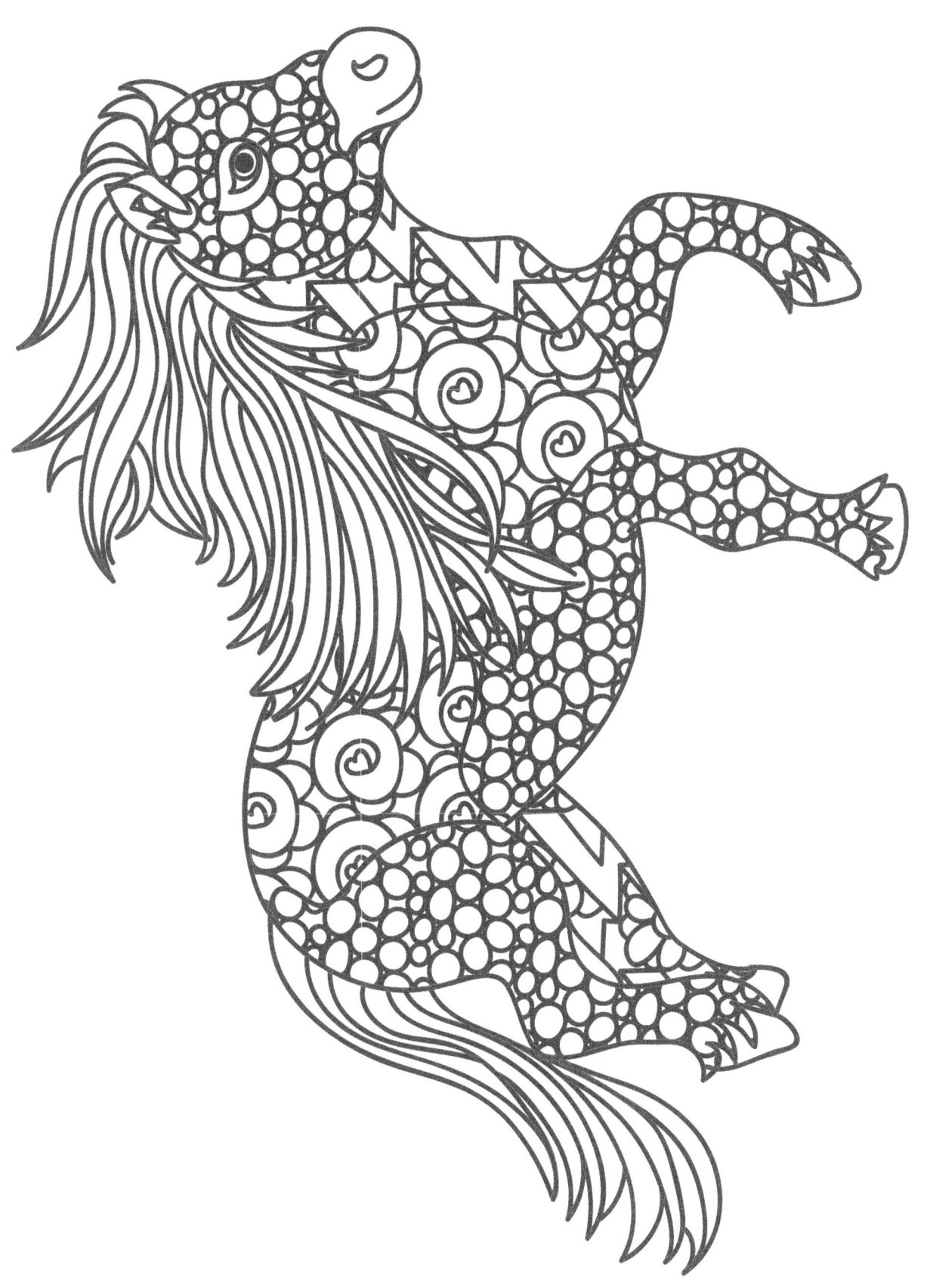

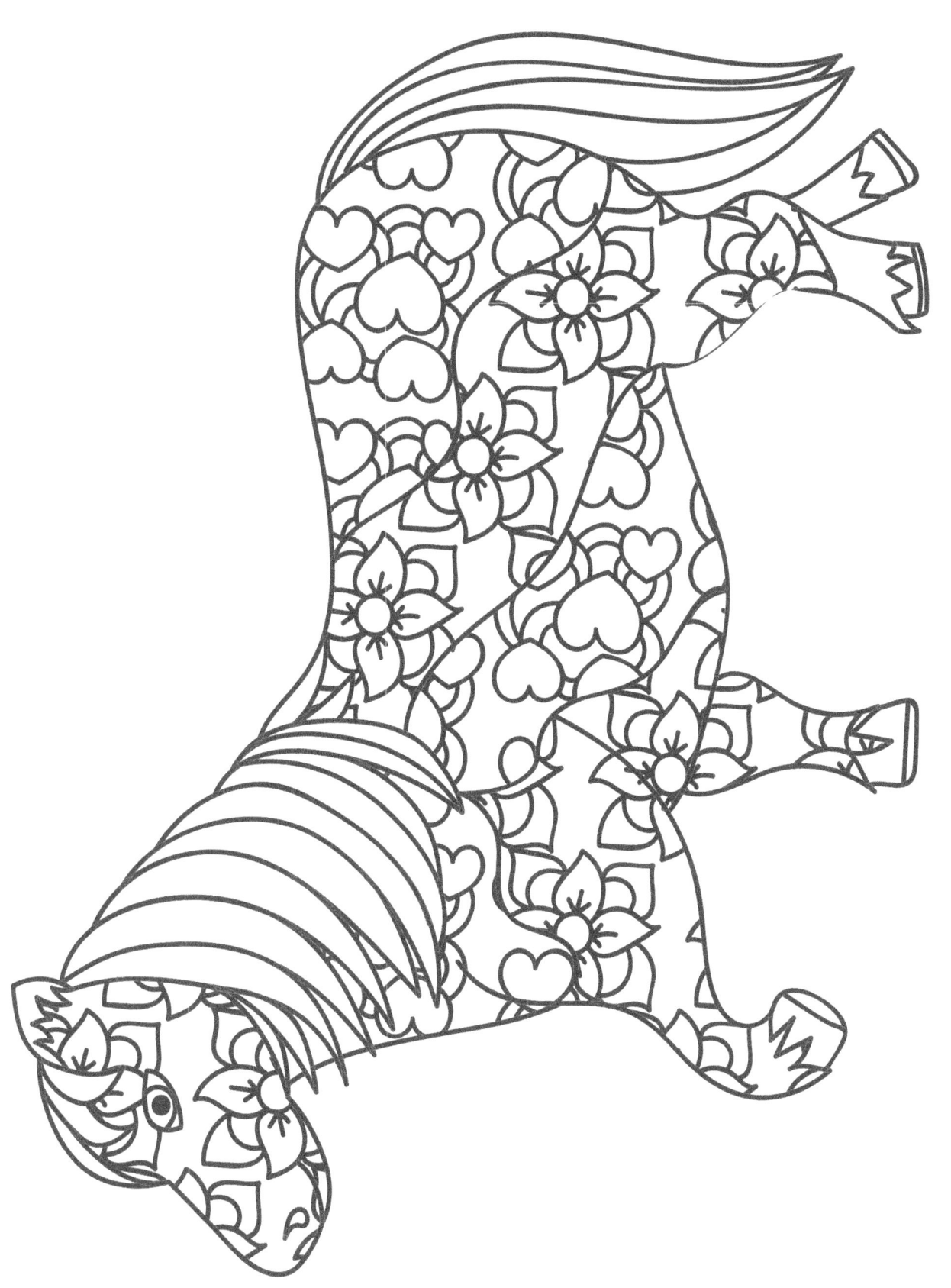

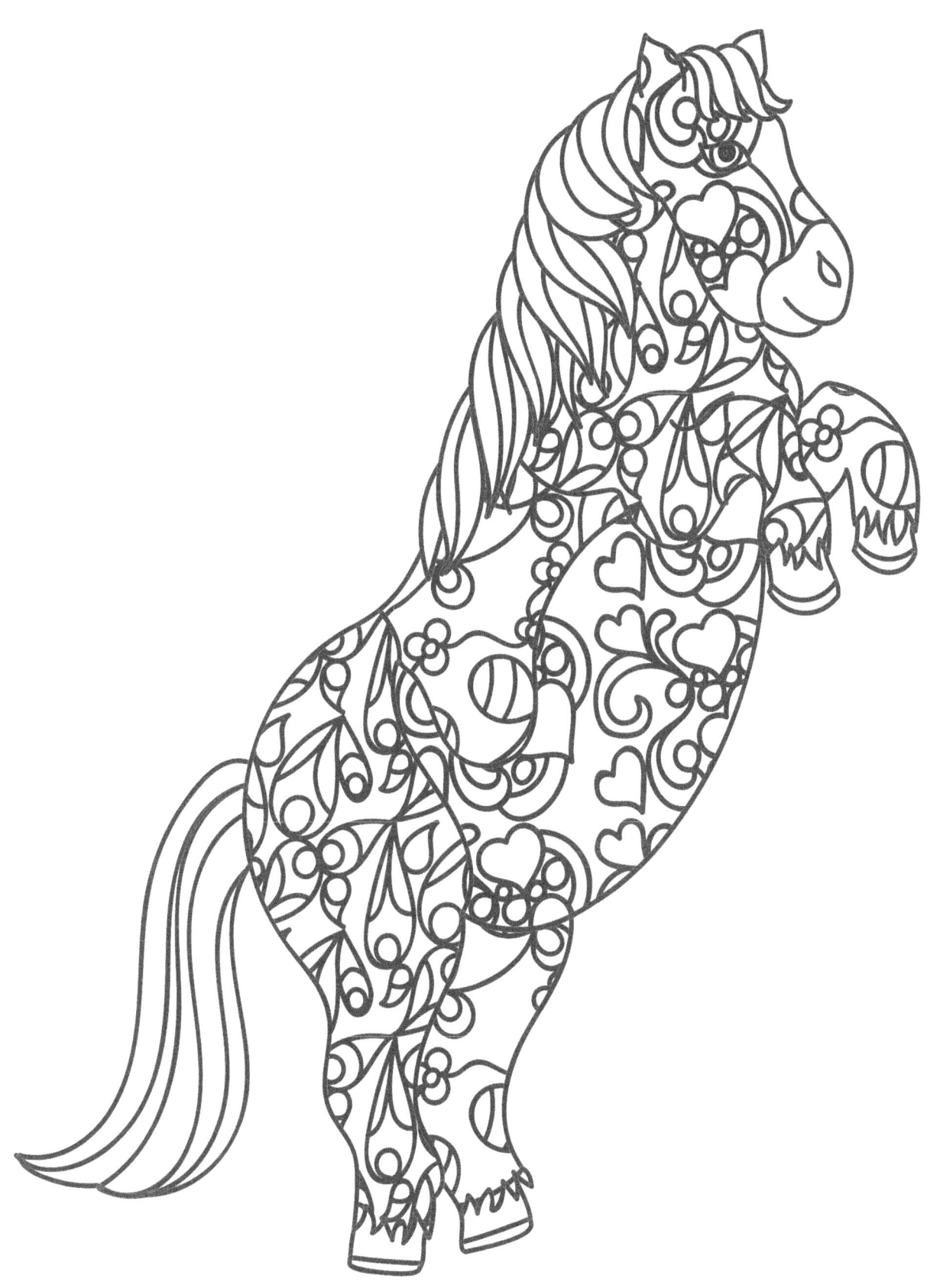

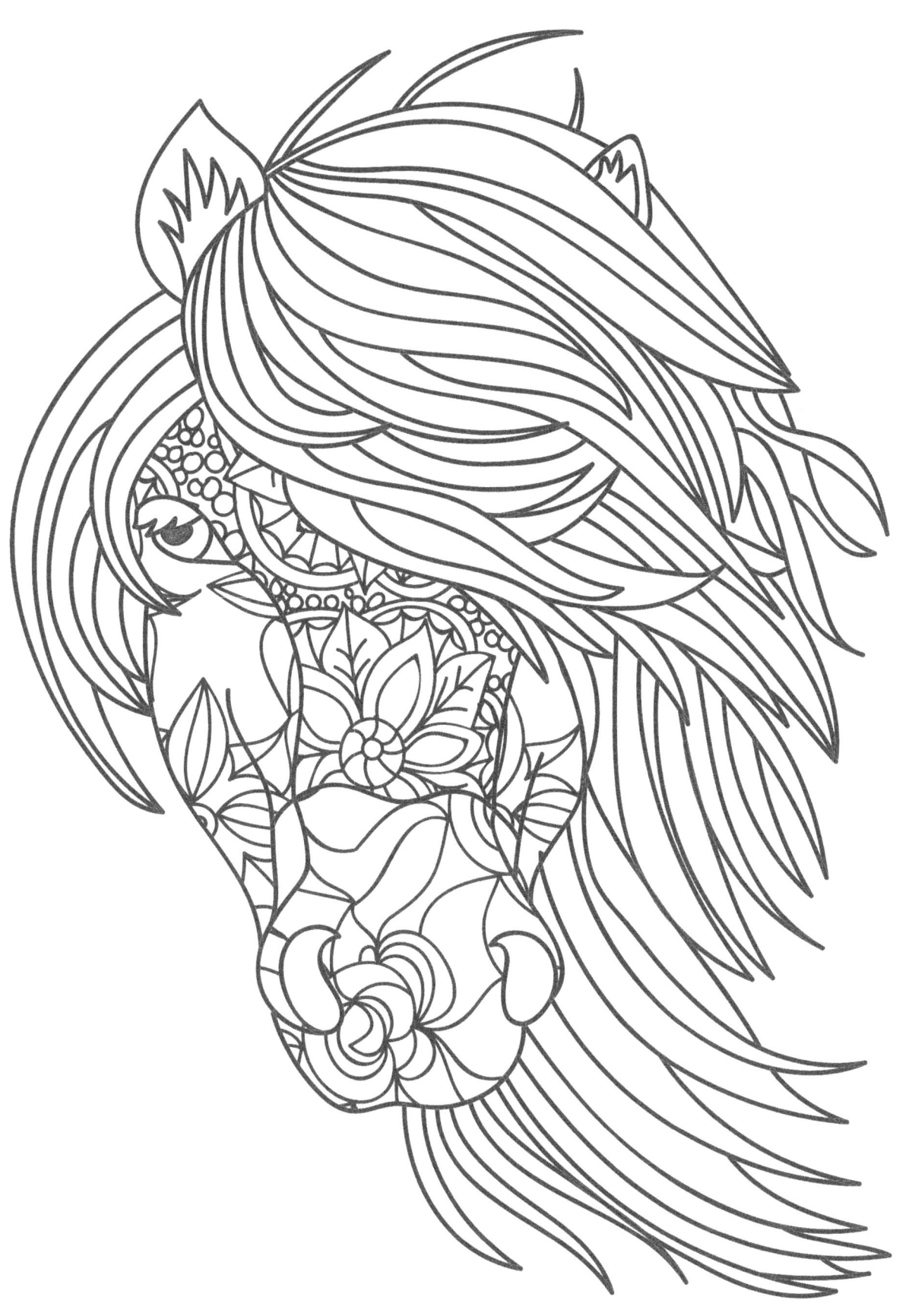

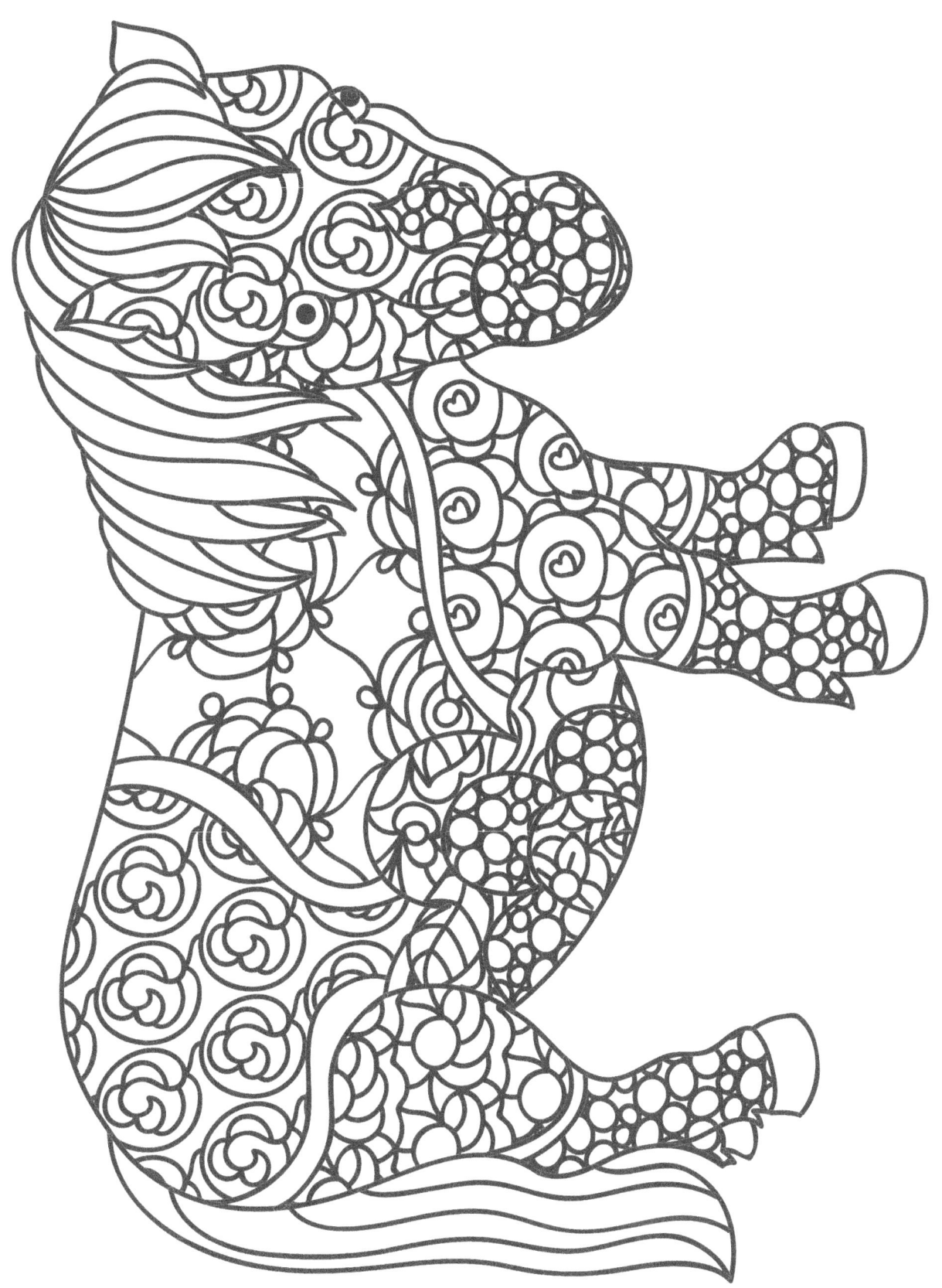

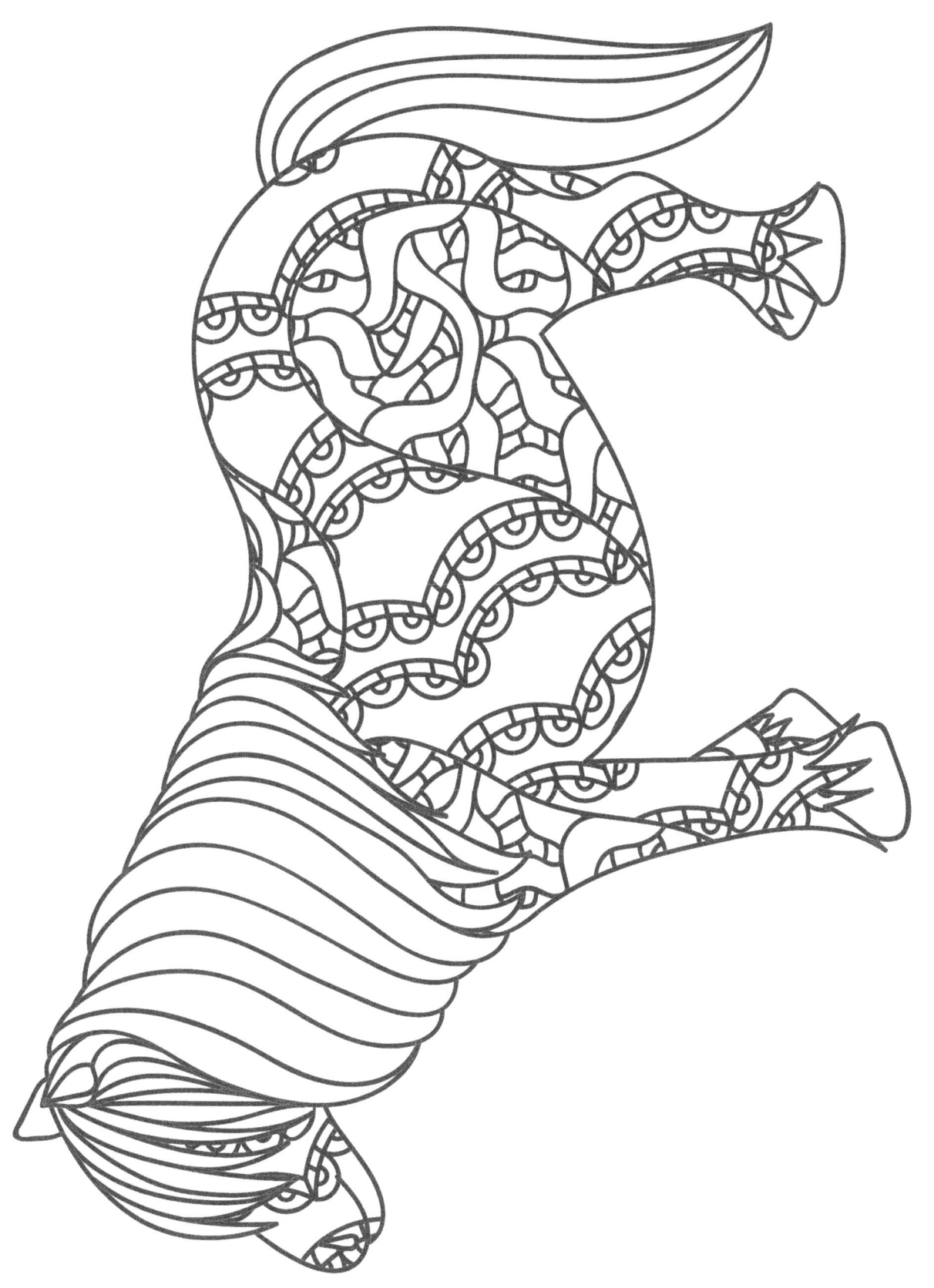

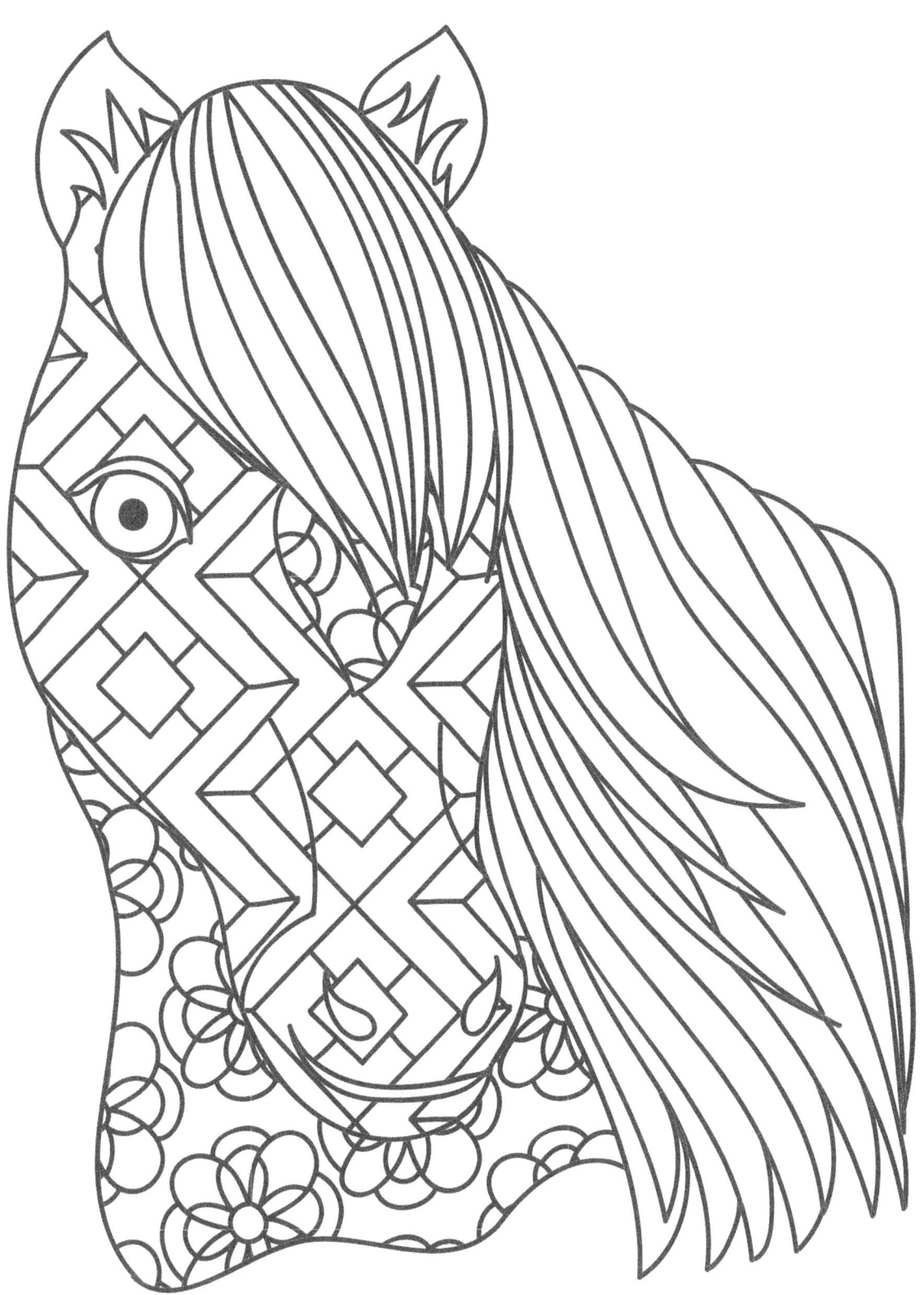

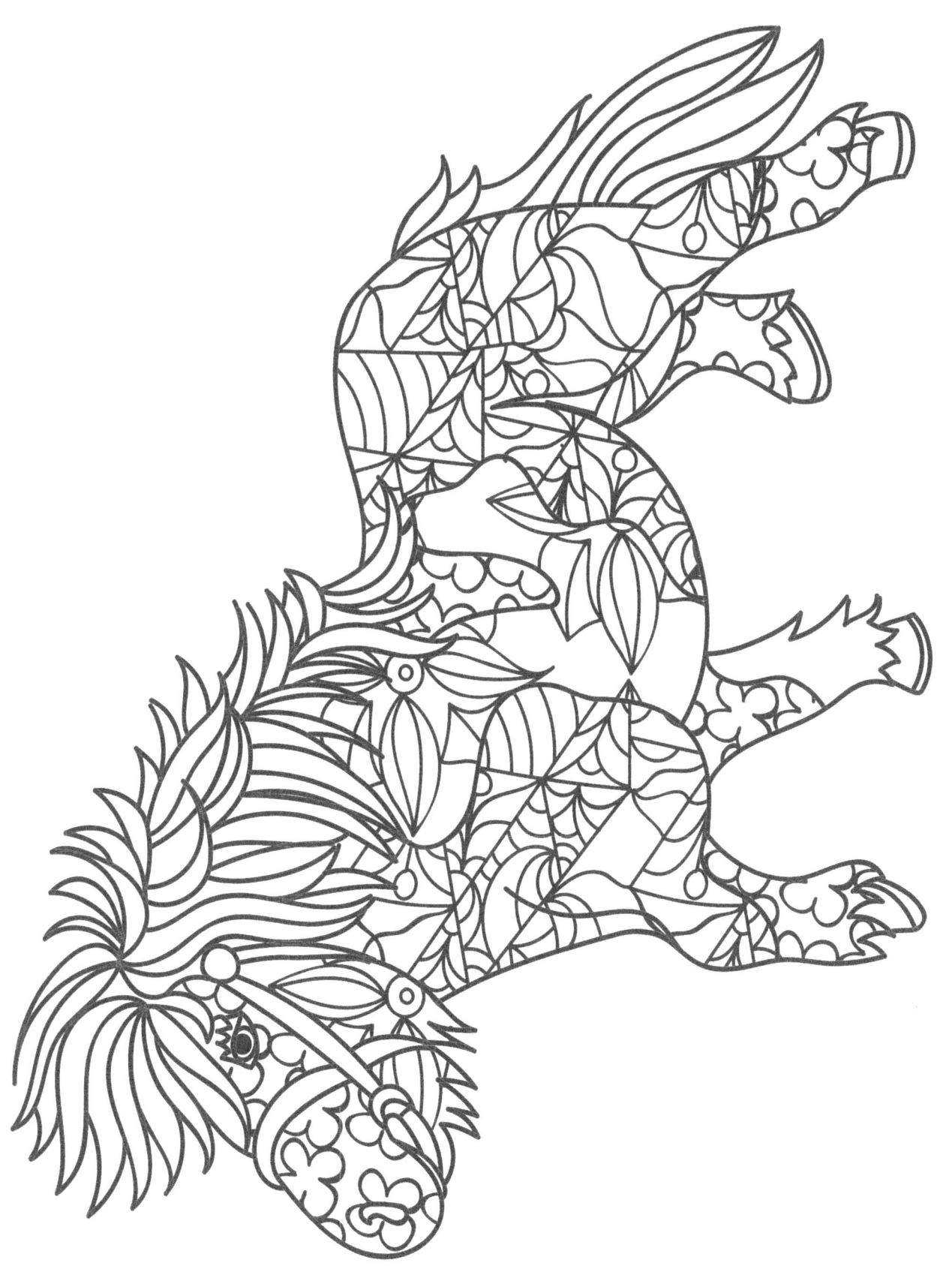

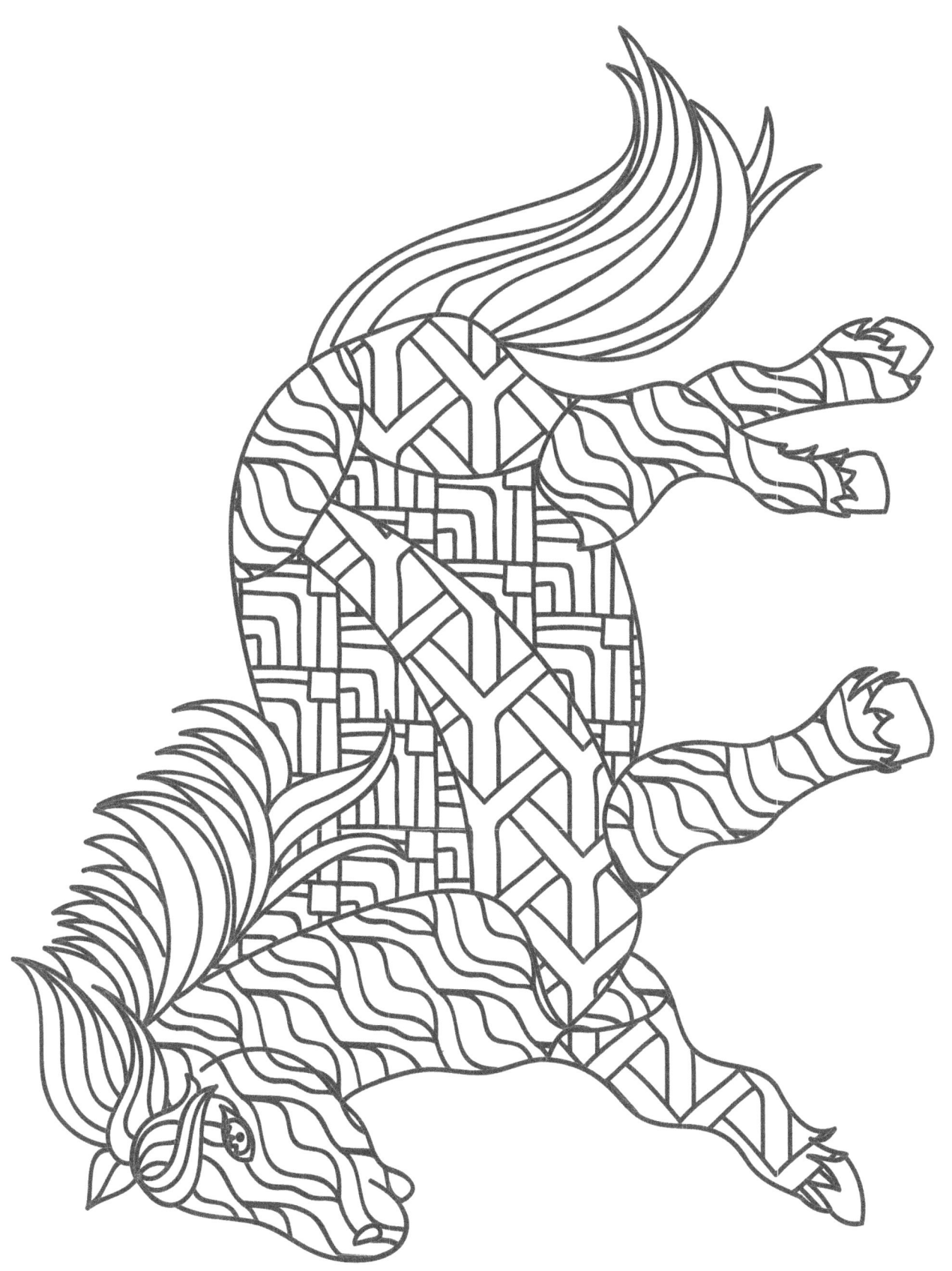

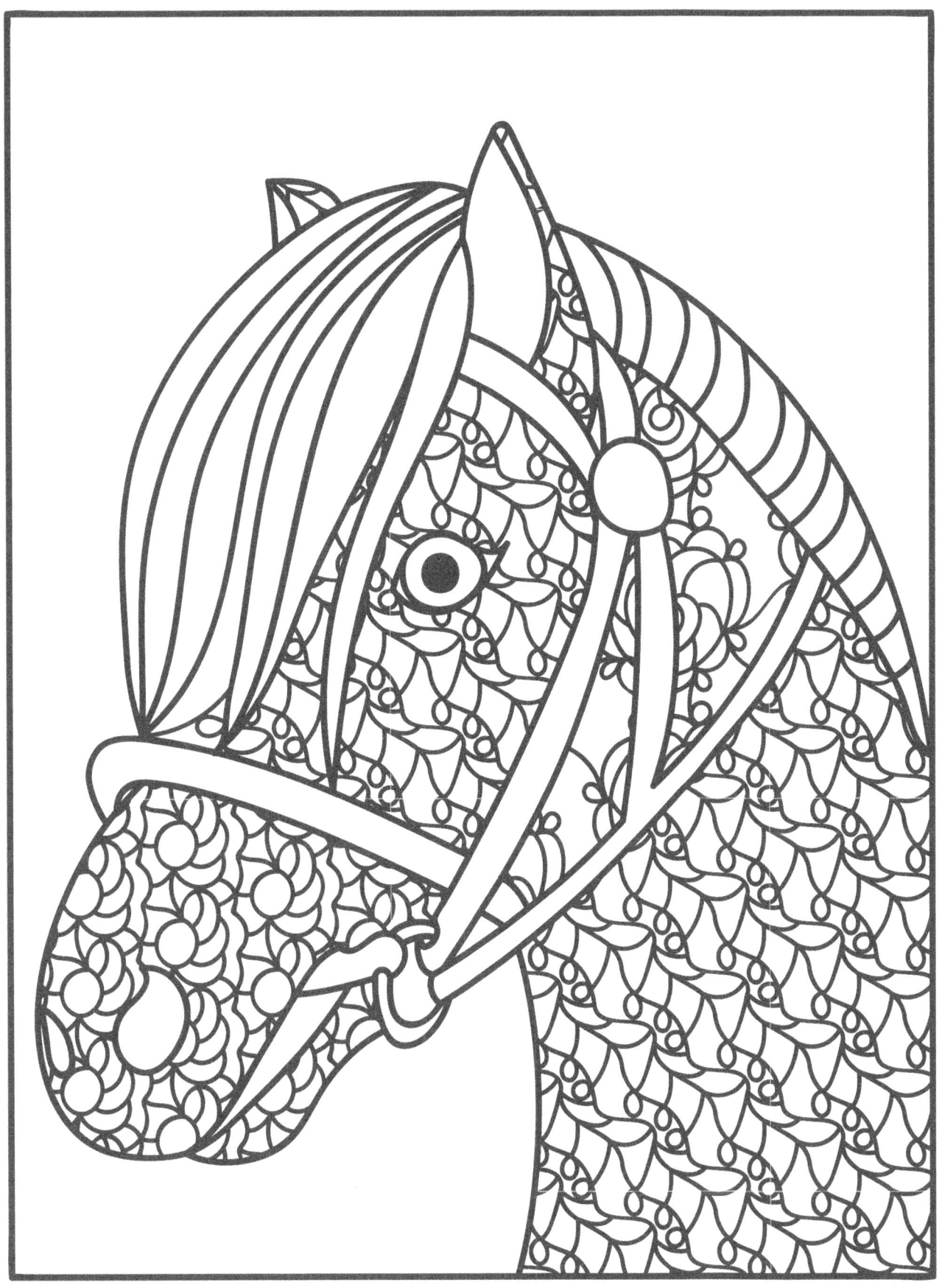

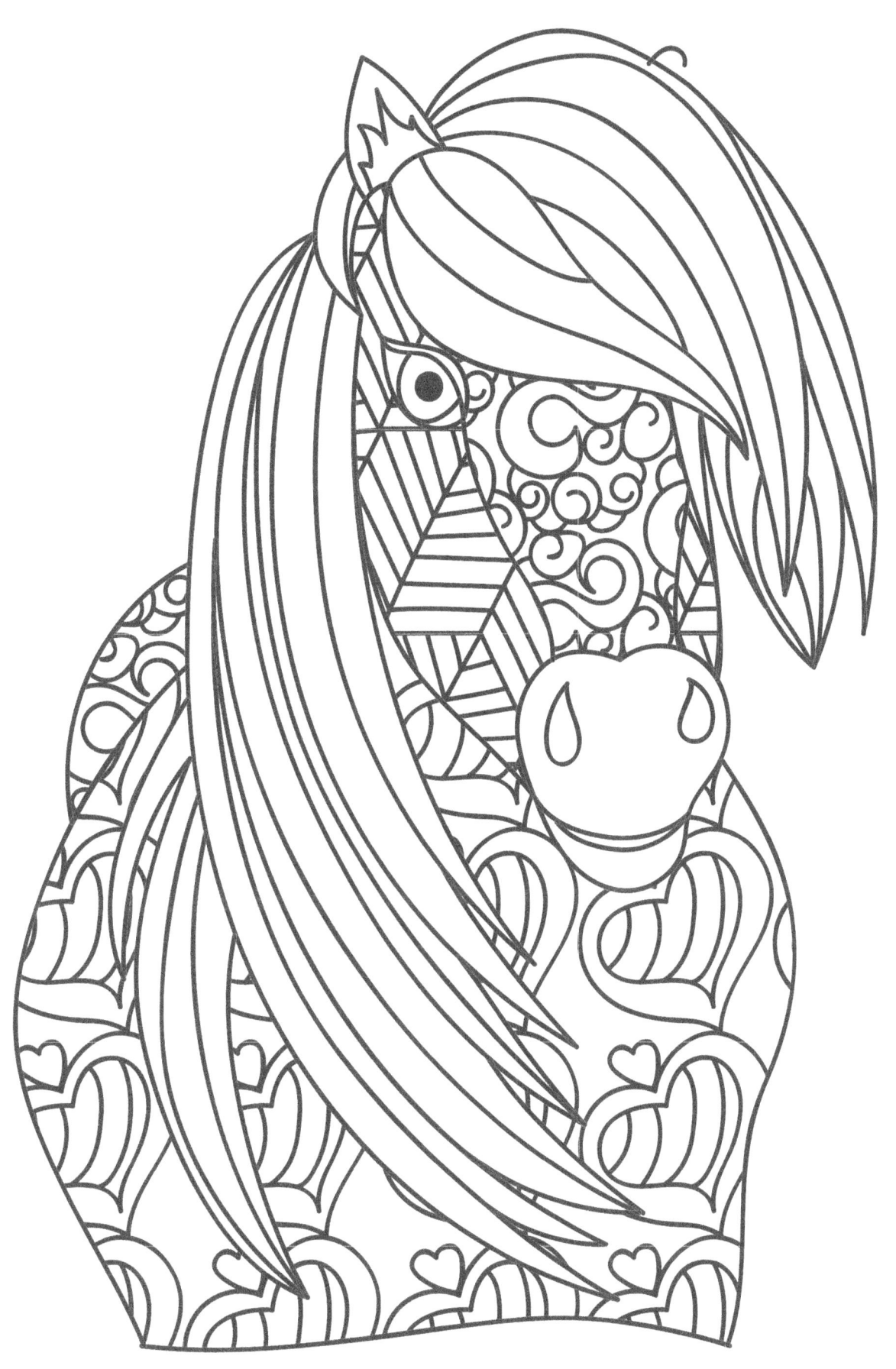

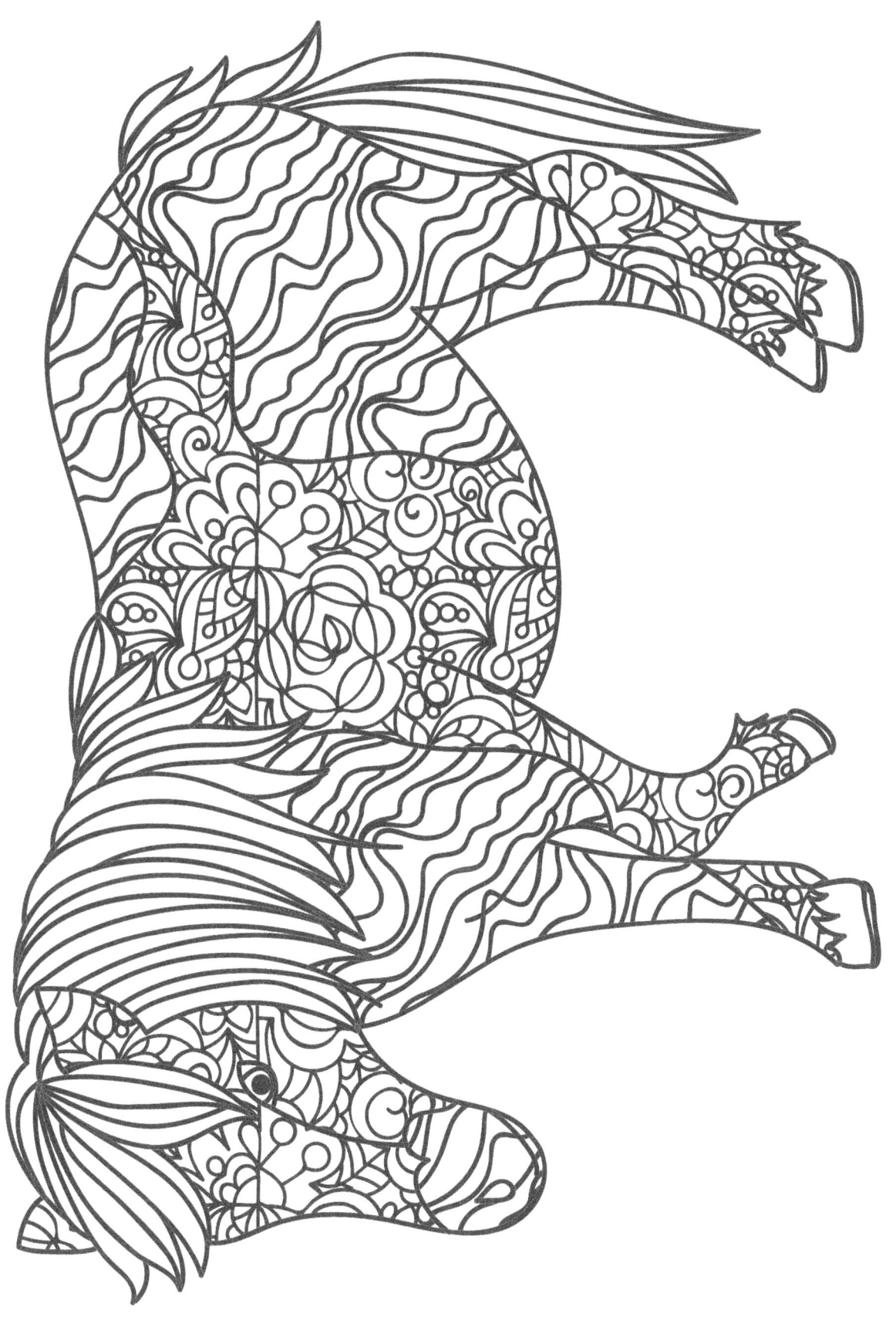

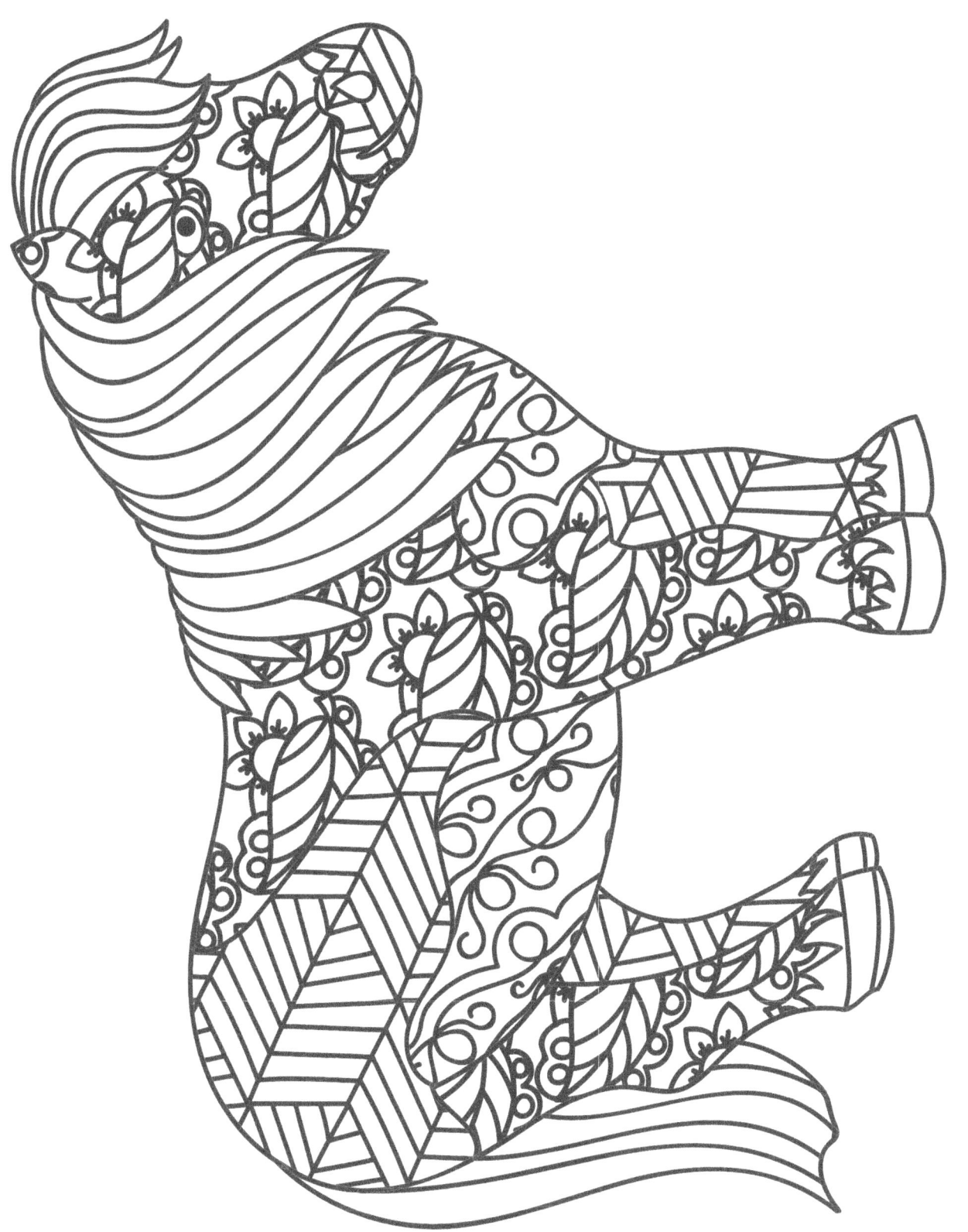

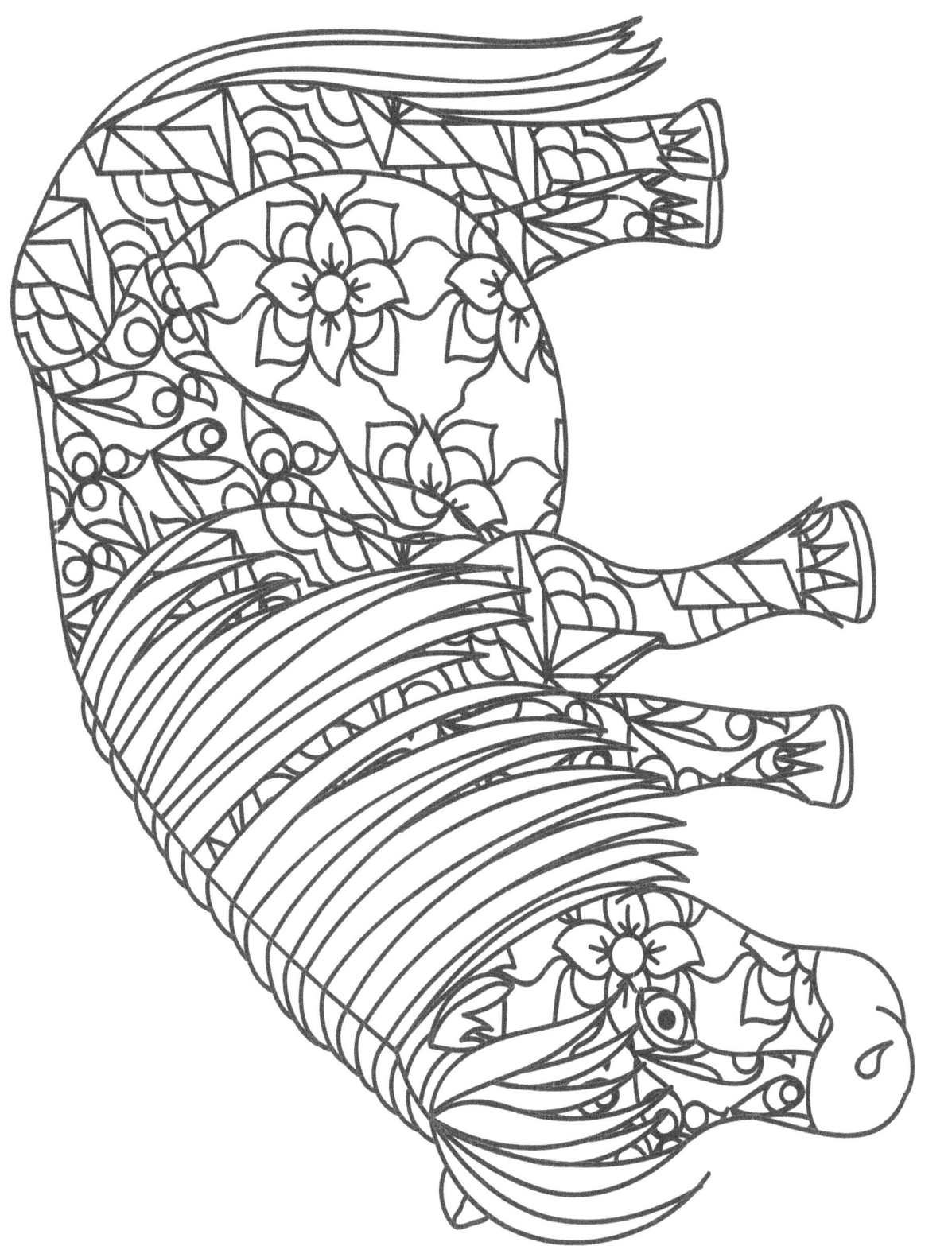

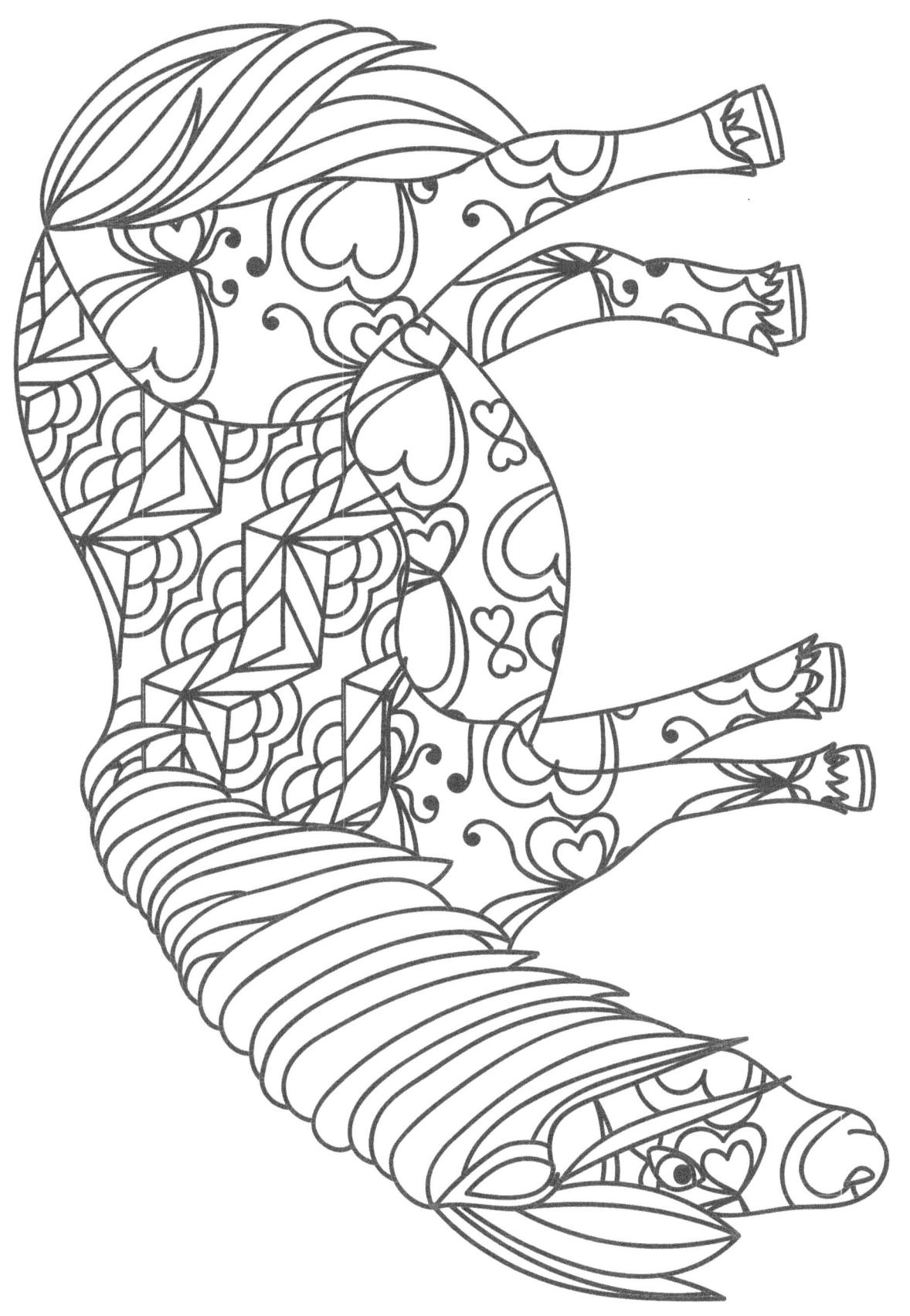

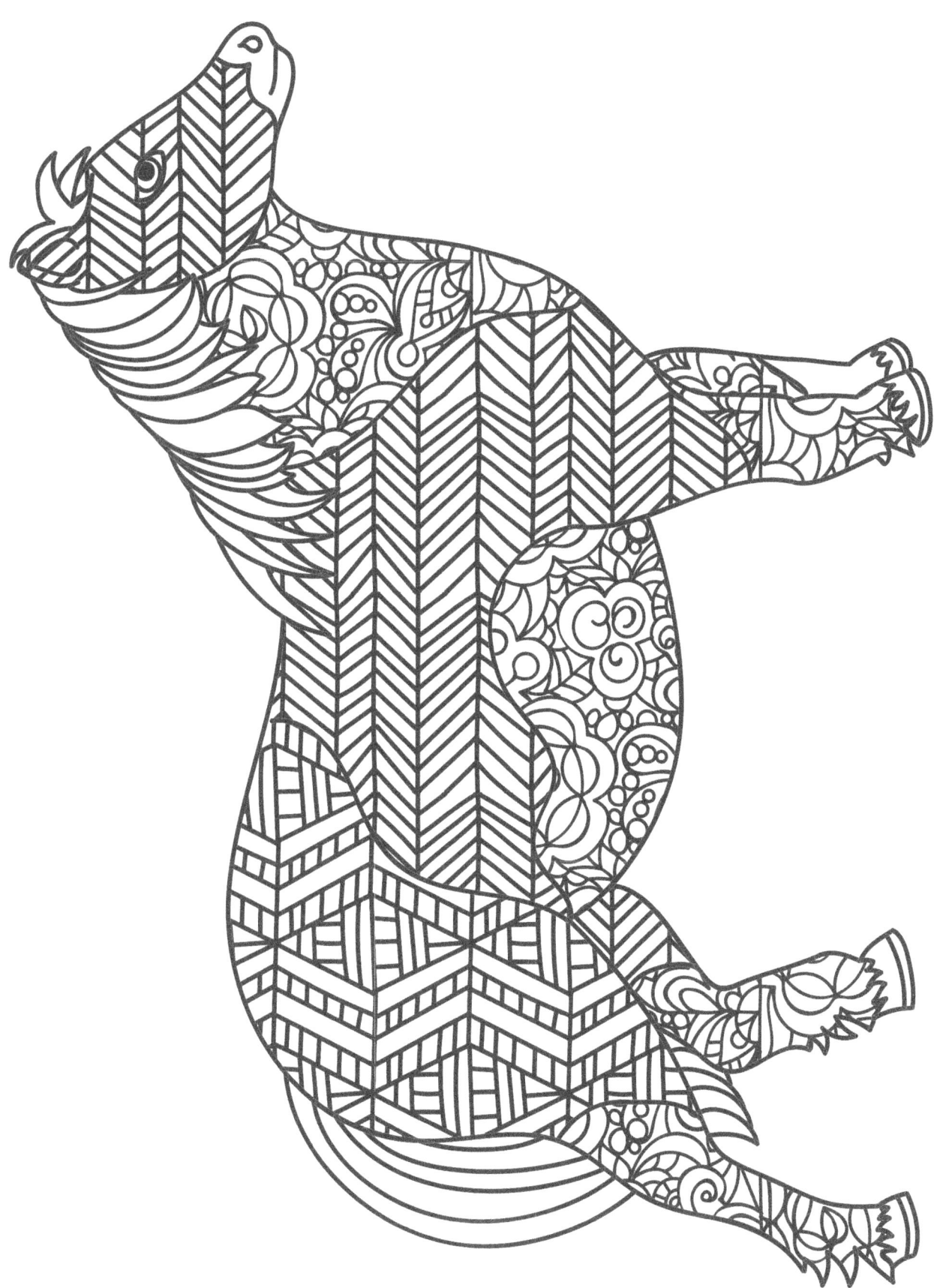

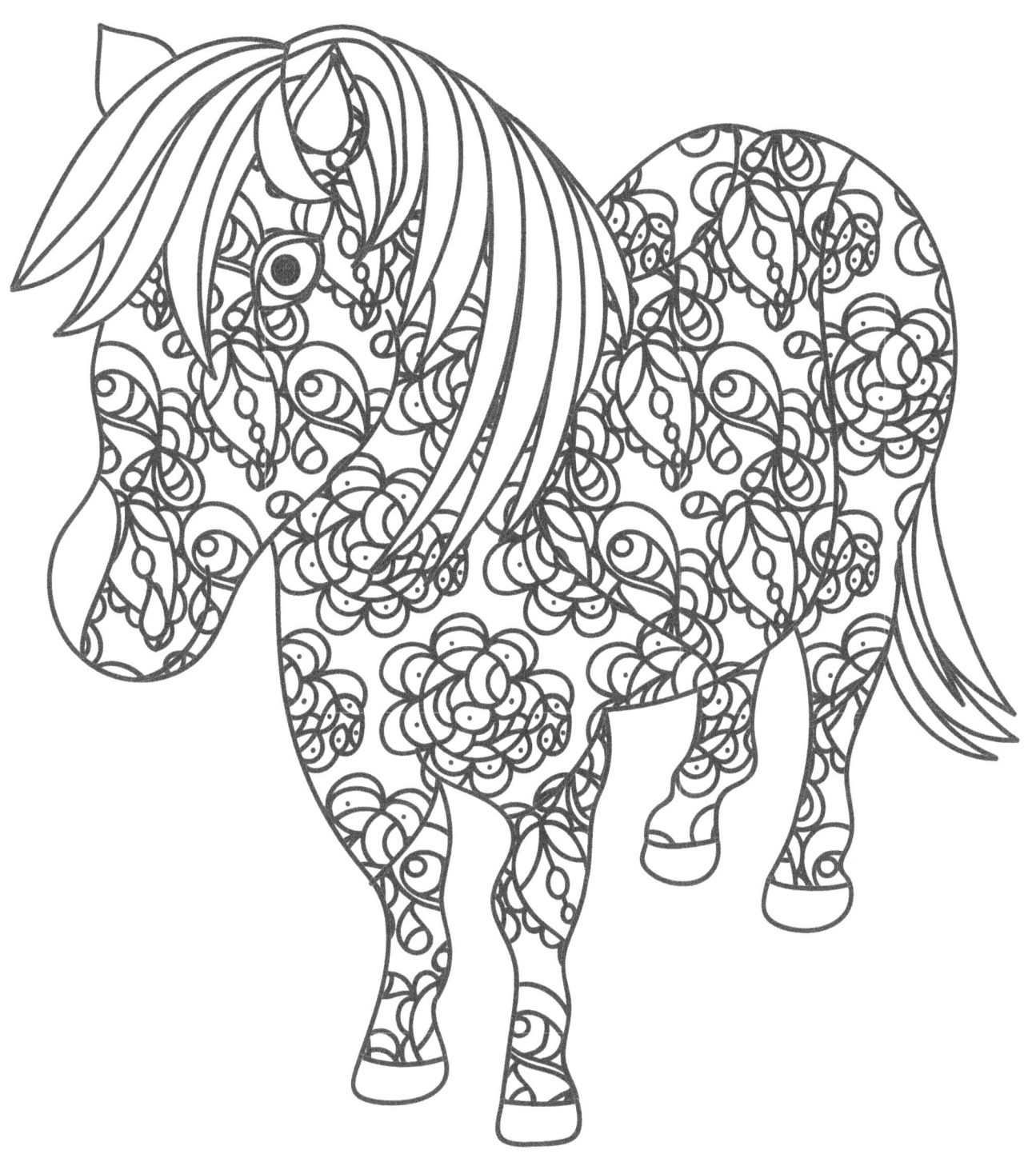

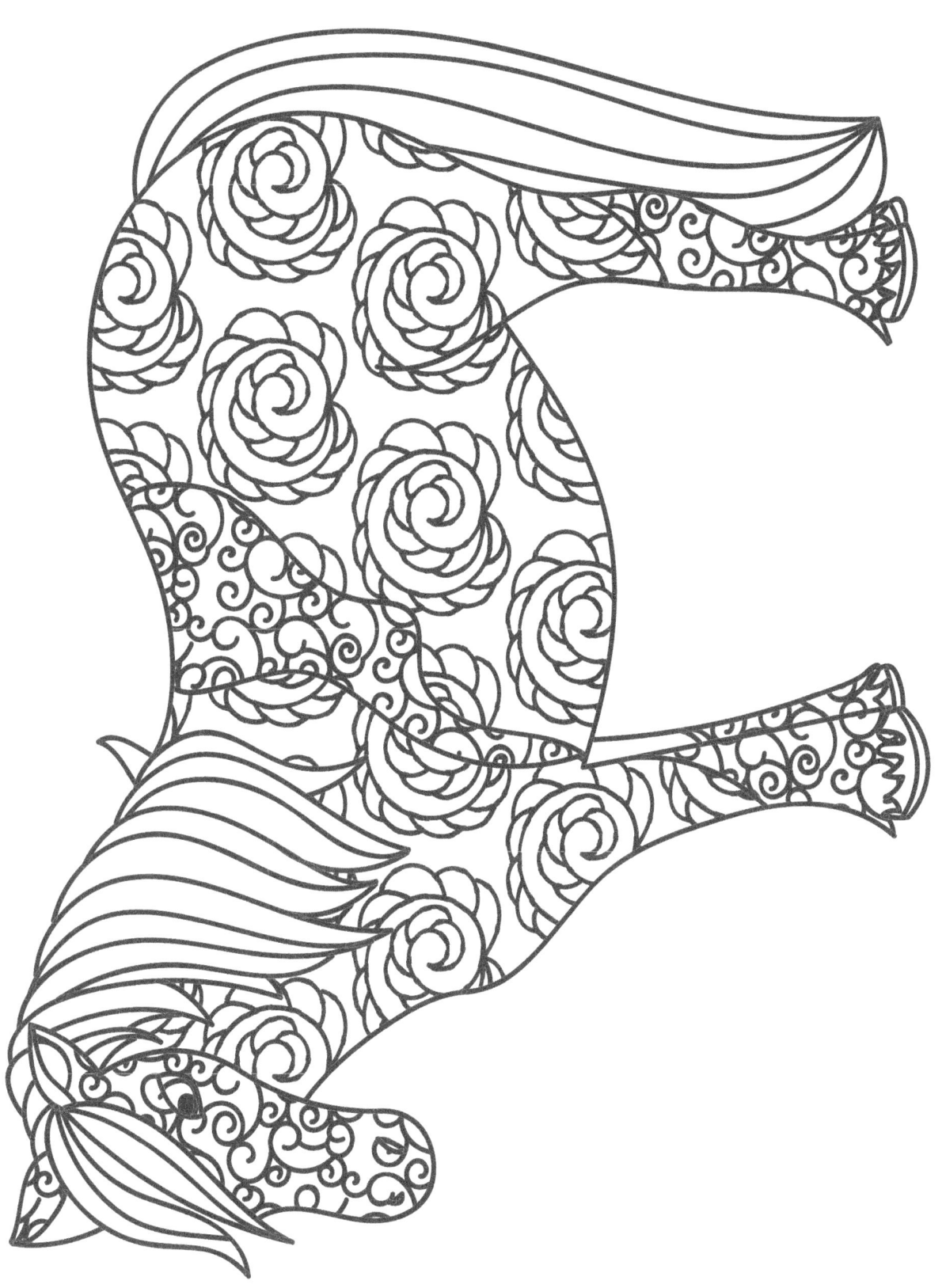

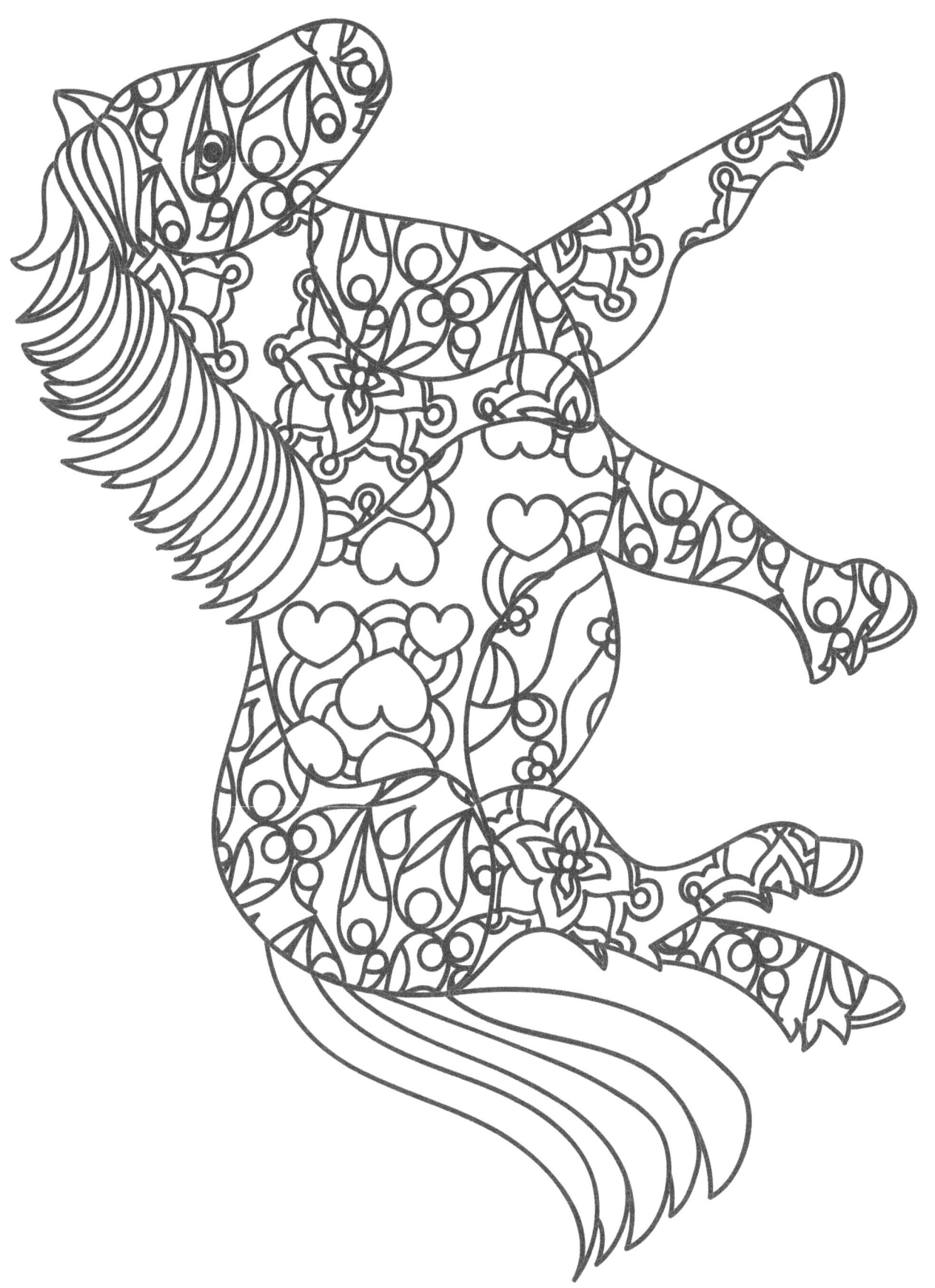

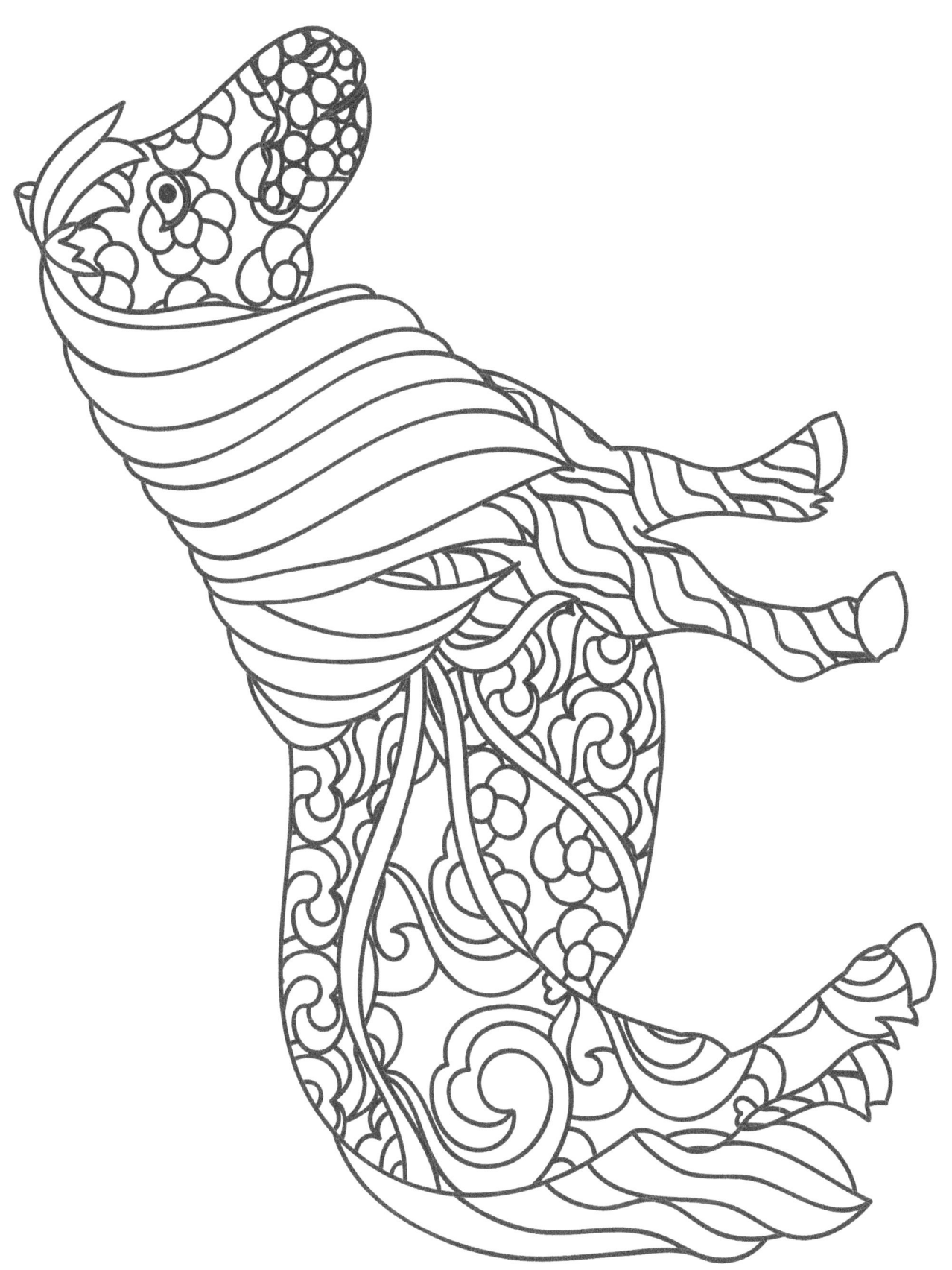

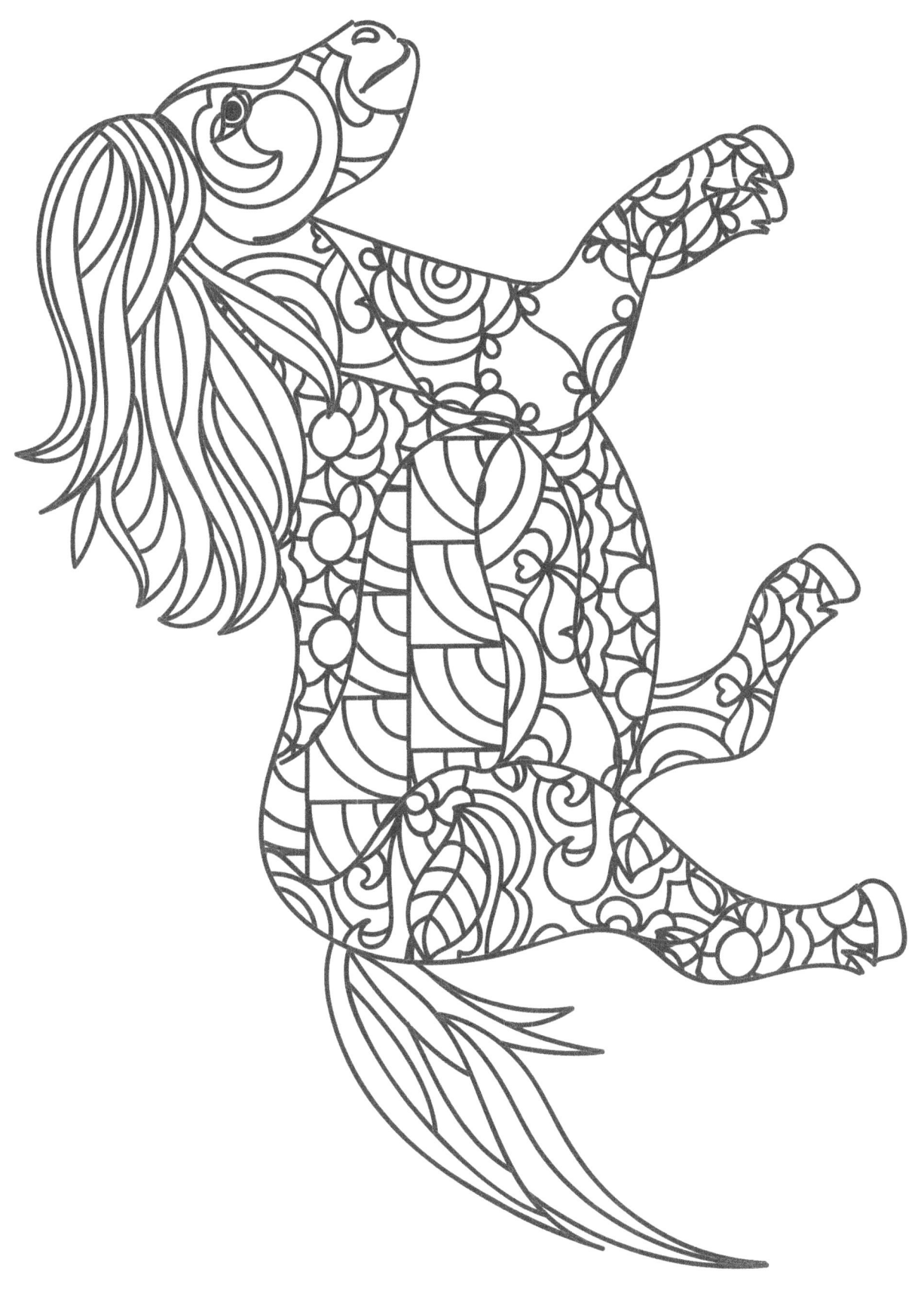

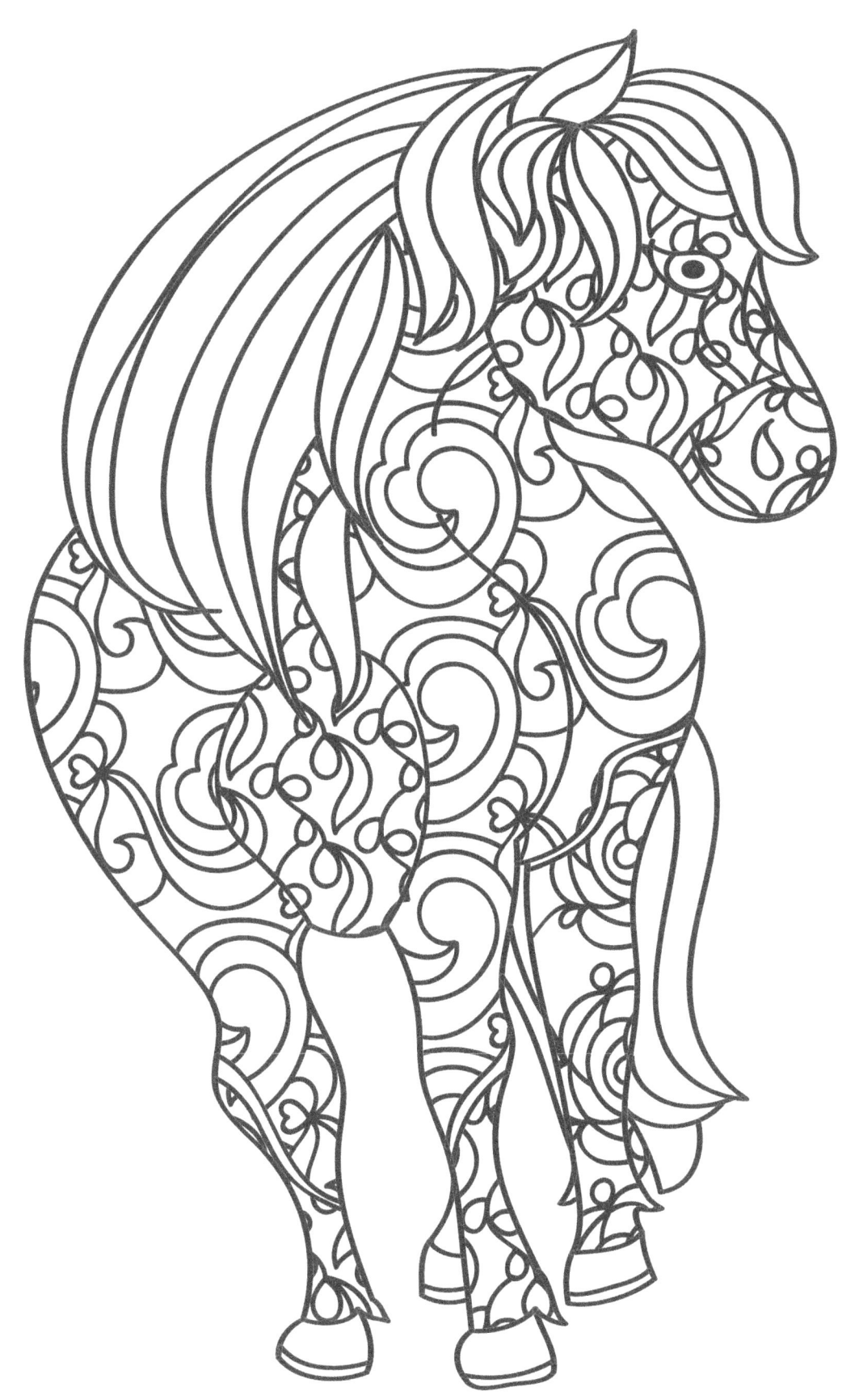

COLOR TEST PAGE

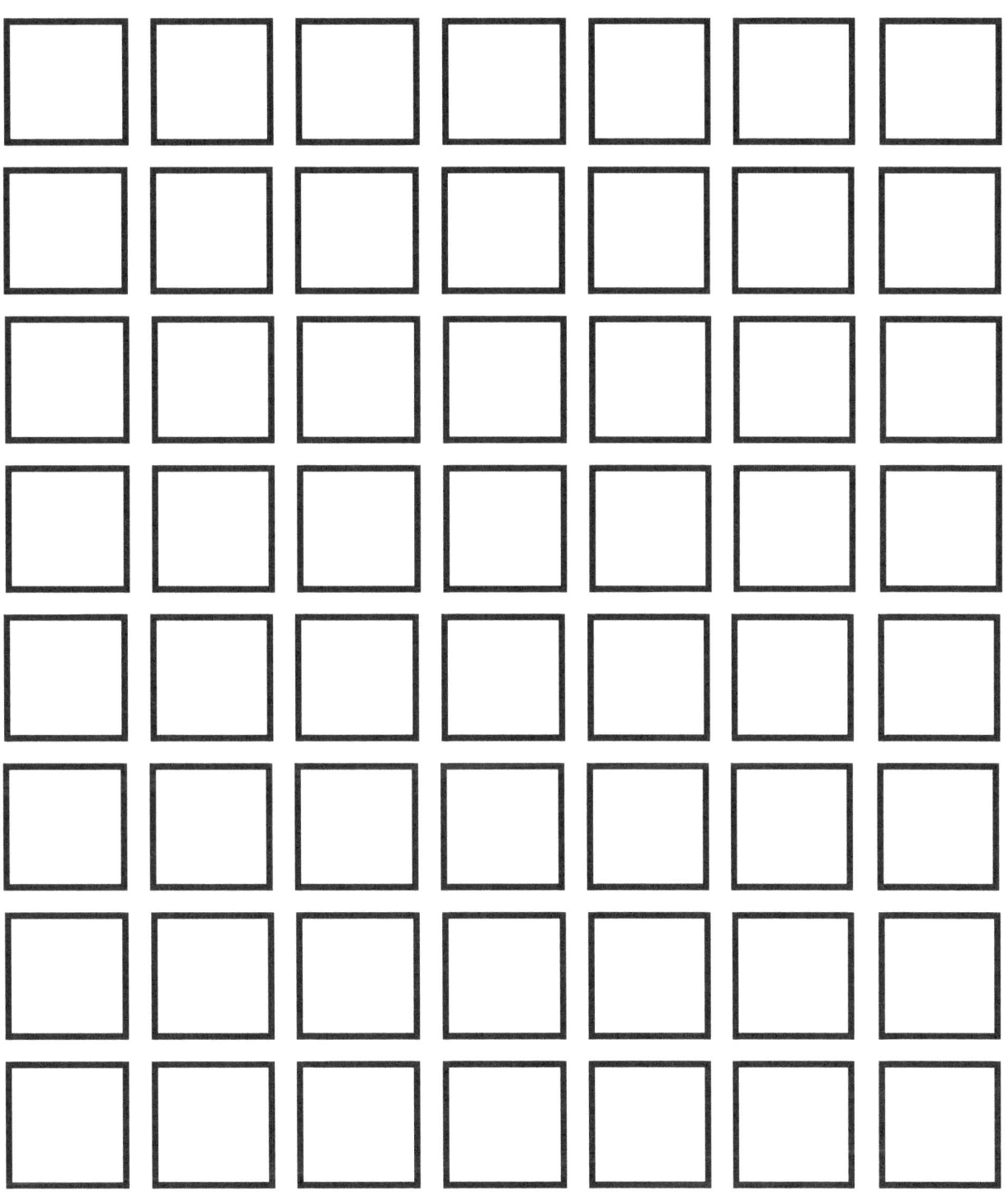

COLOR TEST PAGE

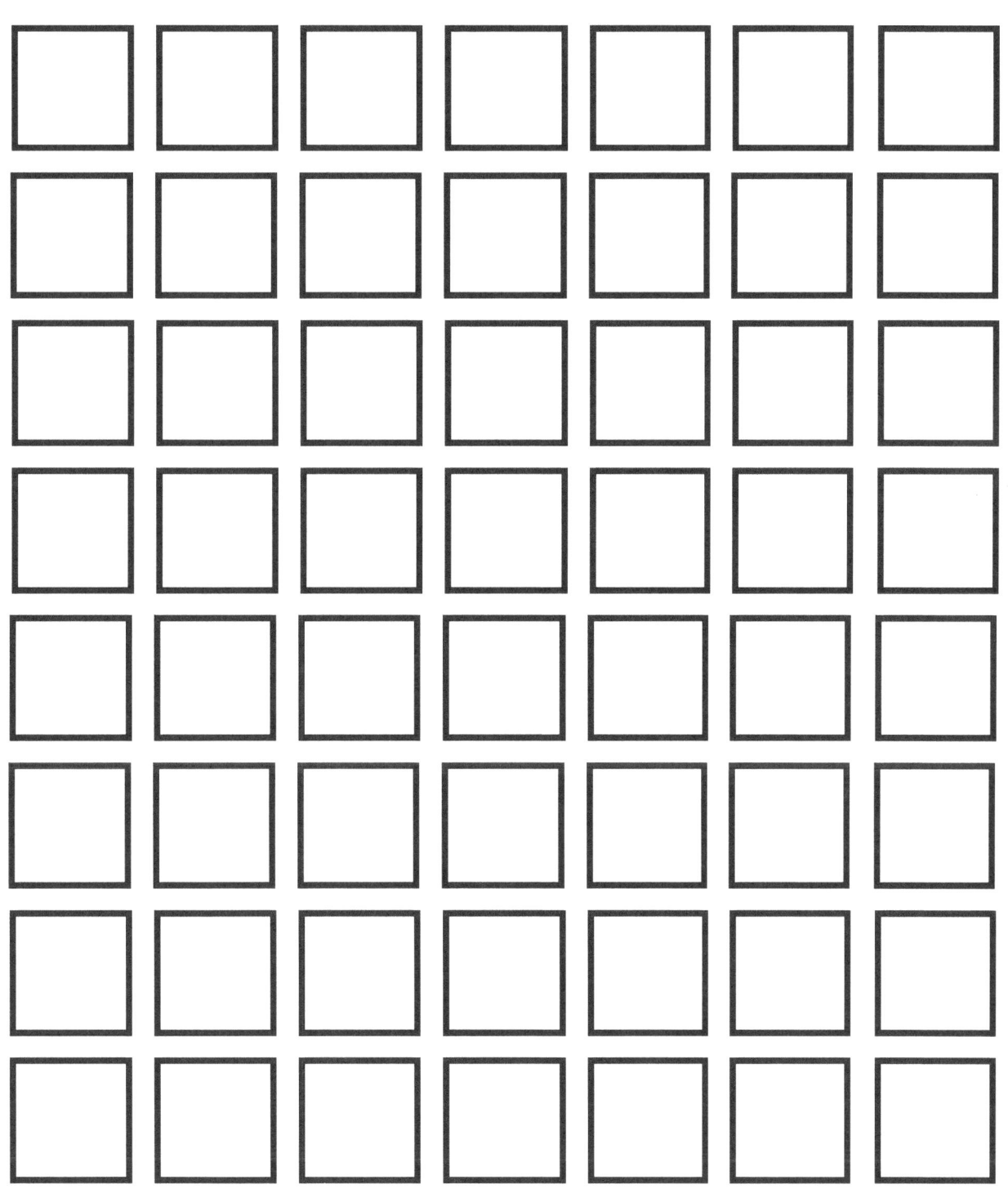

www.ingramcontent.com/pod-product-compliance
Lightning Source LLC
Chambersburg PA
CBHW082255220526
45469CB00009B/3009